Heidegger

Heidegger

A Critical Introduction

Peter Trawny

Translated by Rodrigo Therezo

polity

First published in German as *Martin Heidegger. Eine kritische Einführung*
© Vittorio Klostermann GmbH, Frankfurt am Main, 2016

This English edition © Polity Press, 2019

The translation of this work was funded by Geisteswissenschaften International –
Translation Funding for Work in the Humanities and Social Sciences from
Germany, a joint initiative of the Fritz Thyssen Foundation, the German Federal
Foreign Office, the collecting society VG WORT and the Börsenverein des
Deutschen Buchhandels (German Publishers & Booksellers Association).

Polity Press
65 Bridge Street
Cambridge CB2 1UR, UK

Polity Press
101 Station Landing
Suite 300
Medford, MA 02155, USA

ISBN-13: 978-1-5095-2175-3
ISBN-13: 978-1-5095-2176-0 (pb)

A catalogue record for this book is available from the British Library.

Library of Congress Cataloging-in-Publication Data

Names: Trawny, Peter, 1964- author.
Title: Heidegger : a critical introduction / Peter Trawny.
Other titles: Martin Heidegger. English
Description: Cambridge ; Medford, MA : Polity, [2018] | English translation of:
    Martin Heidegger : eine kritische Einführung. | Includes bibliographical references
    and index.
Identifiers: LCCN 2018024450 (print) | LCCN 2018034840 (ebook) | ISBN
    9781509521791 (Epub) | ISBN 9781509521753 | ISBN
    9781509521753q(hardback) | ISBN 9781509521760q(paperback)
Subjects: LCSH: Heidegger, Martin, 1889-1976.
Classification: LCC B3279.H49 (ebook) | LCC B3279.H49 T64513 2018 (print) |
    DDC 193–dc23
LC record available at https://lccn.loc.gov/2018024450

Typeset in 10.5 on 12 pt Sabon by Toppan Best-set Premedia Limited
Printed and bound in the UK by CPI Group (UK) Ltd, Croydon

For further information on Polity, visit our website: politybooks.com

Contents

Preface to the English Edition

After the translation of my book *Heidegger and the Myth of a Jewish World Conspiracy*, for which I thank Andrew Mitchell,[1] it is now my *Critical Introduction* to Heidegger's thought that is here translated into English.

Since the publication of the *Black Notebook*s and the intense controversy that their anti-Semitic statements provoked in Europe, the discussion of Heidegger's thought has been inscribed in a political context. The willingness to read the master of soil and rootedness in a critical manner has given rise to a fiercely defensive attitude from supporters of the nation and Christianity. One wants to protect the master: we had already forgiven him for a bit of anti-Semitism before he made himself even more explicit on this point.

At the other end of the spectrum, we find judges who seem to have been personally appointed by morality itself and who wish to purify the academy of all evil – as if the very idea of "purification" were not itself affected by this evil. These warriors for peace want the best of all possible worlds. In such a world, Heidegger's thought still has a place only as an example of evil.

In the antagonism between immediate supporter and immediate critic, it is not difficult to recognize the major political tendencies of our age. It concerns the darkest circle of racists as well as the most enlightened advocates of gender theory:

the more the former deeply hates the other, the more the latter wants universal respect for the other. The severity of one's own position is derived from the severity of the other side's position. We must interpret the current political debates in a dialectical manner.

Both sides consider my own position to be untenable. To recognize problems in Heidegger's thought, without wishing to extricate this thought from the history of philosophy, seems to be inconsequential. What is more, whoever still considers this thought to be a vital source for philosophizing in our day and age will immediately be seen as an accomplice of the condemned.

I cannot but disagree with this view. Yes, we can learn from Heidegger how to think. This thinking discloses paths and unknown regions in which we can experience philosophy pure and simple, i.e., the act of philosophizing as the movement of thought. Nevertheless, this thinking also goes astray in unspeakably trivial ways, that is to say, not only by making "great" mistakes.[2] *The Experience of Thinking Itself*: this is perhaps the title under which I would like to unfold what I have to say about Heidegger's philosophy in my Introduction. A world trapped in its own immaterial webs is in need of this experience.

Peter Trawny
Berlin, February 15, 2018

Introduction

I profit from a philosopher only insofar as he can be an
example.[1]

Friedrich Nietzsche

"Paths – not works," writes Heidegger at the beginning of
the collected edition of his works (*Gesamtausgabe*) that extends
to more than a hundred volumes.[2] In this way, Heidegger
wishes to point to the open and performative character of his
thinking. Among his texts we find *Off the Beaten Track* (*Holzwege*) and *Pathmarks* (*Wegmarken*).[3] *On the Way to Language*
(*Unterwegs zur Sprache*) is his philosophy.[4] *The Country Path*
is particularly dear to the thinker.[5] The use of the plural "paths"
indicates that his thinking does not know a unique path that
would culminate in an "oeuvre."

For Heidegger, thinking has a "path-like character," i.e., it
has more to do with its actual carrying out than with the
production of an "oeuvre."[6] "I hold no brief for my philosophy, precisely because I do not have a philosophy of my own,"
says Heidegger during a lecture course.[7] For Heidegger, philosophy is nothing one could "have." Philosophy takes place
(*ereignet sich*): it is to experience the world in a reflective
manner, "to make way for it," that is, "to provide paths for
it."[8] In this understanding of philosophy, it is not at all certain
that these paths will lead to truth. On the contrary, a philosophy that is on the way can go astray.

"Woodpaths" (*Holzwege*) are a kind of "aberrant path" (*Irrweg*); they come to an end inside the forest, leading nowhere. "Pathmarks" (*Wegmarken*) are points of orientation along such paths. It is not easy to find one's way. This is why Heidegger's thinking goes astray along wayward paths. It belongs to the peculiar pathos of this philosophy not to shy away from what is false, far away, and even obscure. This problematic pathos according to which it is possible for thought to err – given that we can never be absolutely certain that we are always "on the right path" – is a source of irritation that Heidegger's philosophy stirs up time and again. On the one hand, Heidegger is considered to be one of the few truly important philosophers of the twentieth century; for the physicist Carl Friedrich von Weizsäcker, he is "perhaps *the* philosopher of the twentieth century."[9] On the other hand, Heidegger is massively rejected by many critics. Ultimately, this rejection does not hinge on Heidegger's irremediable error of getting lost in National Socialism.

"The depth of a *philosophy* is measured – in case there is measurement here – by its power to be errant," writes Heidegger in an entry from *Ponderings VII*, one of his so-called *Black Notebooks*.[10] In early 2014, the publication of a number of these notebook entries caused an earthquake in the reception of Heidegger's thought. Though it had long been known that Heidegger decided to become involved with National Socialism in the early 1930s, no one knew that he had also, sporadically and privately, accorded philosophical importance to anti-Semitism. This is precisely what the entries of the *Black Notebooks* from 1938–48 attest.

Therefore, an introduction to Martin Heidegger's philosophy necessarily introduces us to his anti-Semitism. Wouldn't it be better, then, not to write such an introduction at all? Instead, shouldn't we be advising others against such a "philosophy"? Shouldn't we banish it into history's "poison cabinet"? Should access to it be granted only to those who are educated enough to recognize its errors?

As concerns the core of the anti-Semitic statements that surface in Heidegger's thinking, we must present them in a clear and lucid manner. In a certain way, this presentation will already be an interpretation that we must likewise underscore in a particular manner. This interpretation will focus on Heidegger's notebook entries concerning the Jews – entries that are, in many regards, highly problematic and absurd (*Abwegige*). As opposed to other interpreters, my view is not that Heidegger's entire thinking is to be characterized as anti-Semitic. I have thoroughly revised my 2003 introduction because I could no longer leave it as written after coming to know the *Black Notebooks*.

We cannot, however, reduce what is troublesome and provocative about Heidegger's thinking to his misguided worldviews and political errancies. Rather, the causes for this are many, and they seem to be the same sources that triggered and still continue to trigger fervent admiration as well as bitter contempt for this thinker. At age seventy-one, Hans-Georg Gadamer, one of Heidegger's most influential students, recognized that he was much indebted to his teacher. He then very tellingly adds: "[...] and I also know very well that it is precisely my tendency towards moderation – an ultimate indecisiveness almost raised to a (hermeneutical) principle – that makes me accessible and tolerable, whereas your original engagement is inaccessible and passes as intolerable."[11] Heidegger's thinking is anything but moderate. The philosopher is familiar with extremes and does not mince words: he takes what is most extreme as the norm and has no desire to think any differently. Time and again, not only does he thematize the "decisions" and "ruptures," the profound caesuras and horrors of existence, but also that which heals, with which every life is acquainted. And is it not the case that wars and genocides have affected life in an extreme way during the two halves of the twentieth century? Yes, certainly: for philosophers – men and women – the singularity of the twentieth century lies in the fact that they must necessarily respond to its events, the two world wars, the Shoah, the revolutions. There is no other century in European history whose catastrophes have gripped philosophy in such an ineluctable way. Heidegger's thinking, too, takes a stance vis-à-vis the catastrophes of that century and has thus become a kind of manifestation of this period.

This, of course, does not mean that Heidegger's provocative thinking relates only to concrete events. We can sense Heidegger's barely masked desire to be provocative when he makes the following scandalous statement in a lecture from 1952: "Science does not think."[12] Didn't he know that this was an affront to many scientists? Wasn't he aware of how he was scolding academic scholars of philosophy who did not wish to be exposed to a permanent self-contradiction? Nevertheless, as provocative as this sentence appears to be, it makes perfect sense when understood in context. With increasing affect, Heidegger again summons a "decision" and declares that we must not tolerate indifference. Is philosophy a modern science or not? From the start, Heidegger stated that philosophy is either the science of all sciences – as Aristotle and Hegel would have it – or is not a science at all. But how is a self-declared scientific philosophy supposed to relate today to a thinking that refuses every demand to justify itself before a (morally) higher authority, let alone institution?

"To think is to thank," says Heidegger in a lecture course from the early 1950s.[13] Thinking is not a science, but a "thanking." This seems to be a dramatic exaggeration, a statement that is also alienating and which we attribute to Heidegger's style that is often considered kitsch. Implicit here is simply the thought that also resonates in the German word for "reason" (*Vernunft*), namely, the notion that thinking is not a spontaneous faculty but depends on what it "apprehends" (*vernimmt*). Again, a "decision" is apparently at stake: does thinking itself fabricate its own thoughts, or does it receive them? Has man invented language or does man originate from language?

Yet the maxim "to think is to thank" can still be understood in a different way. Though many critics are suspicious of Heidegger's prophetic posturing and cringe at his not at all "moderate" tone, finding this admittedly esoteric aspect of his thinking to be off-putting, we may not, however, overlook the fact that no other German philosopher of the last century has had as many important students and different interlocutors. Among Heidegger's students, we could mention Hans-Georg Gadamer, Karl Löwith, Hans Jonas, and Herbert Marcuse. Hannah Arendt learned an enormous amount from her teacher and lover. With Ernst Jünger, Heidegger engaged in a philosophical confrontation. He intensely exchanged ideas with the philosophers Max Scheler and Karl Jaspers. With the former psychoanalyst Medard Boss, he co-founded "Dasein-analysis." Extensive correspondence testifies to friendships with the pedagogue Elisabeth Blochmann and also with Imma von Bodmershof, the widow of his admired Hölderlin editor,

Norbert von Hellingrath. The theologian Rudolf Bultmann learned from Heidegger during the latter's time at Marburg. The Germanists Max Kommerell, Emil Staiger, and Beda Allemann recognized his hermeneutical genius. In a double bind of attraction and rejection, Paul Celan sought to be near him. After the war, Heidegger developed relationships in France with Jean Beaufret and his students; he met the poet René Char. We could still mention many others. If "thinking" is a "thanking," this means that philosophy is a dialogue and that the philosopher must be able to let something be said to him, i.e., that it is more important for the philosopher to be able to listen and answer than to close himself off in a monologue. We must be thankful to the other, because the other – others, as Heidegger would be the first to say – makes it possible for us to think.

Heidegger often insisted that each philosopher has only one question to ask. His was the "question of the meaning of being." This question can only be understood in relation to the beginning of European philosophy with Plato and Aristotle. Heidegger relies on these thinkers when he speaks of "being itself," "beings" or "beings as a whole." However, we must not overlook the fact that, in the first phenomenologico-hermeneutical lecture courses that Heidegger gave as an adjunct professor at Freiburg University, he initially thematized the "facticity of life," i.e., the vital actuality of the human being. Without taking lived life into account, we cannot understand the "question of being." There is, then, something nevertheless accurate about the rough shorthand label of "existential philosophy," which is how Heidegger's thought was initially received. The "question of being" is, so to speak, the question of existence and of life. The "factical" was always in play, even when Heidegger's thinking turned to the "history of being" in the 1930s.

Being and Time, an unfinished book manuscript from 1927, is taken to be Heidegger's first major work. Without a proper study of this text, Heidegger's entire oeuvre remains inaccessible. Here, he presents his thinking as "the Dasein analytic," that is to say, at bottom, as the analysis of "factical life." However, according to his own interpretation, Heidegger thus launched the question "of being itself" by relying too heavily on the perspective of the Dasein that is in each case mine, that is, on a human perspective. It became necessary for Heidegger to modify his thinking.

For the most part, the concept of the "turn" is employed to capture this modification. According to Heidegger's thought after *Being and Time*, questioning no longer has to begin with Dasein but rather with "being itself," so that it can, from there, come back to Dasein's life. However, the division of Heidegger's philosophy into a thinking "before" and "after" the "turn" is misleading. Instead, we must observe that Heidegger is always thinking "at" the "turn," that is to say, he is meditating on the *relation* between "being" and Dasein. When he stresses in a few texts that he wants to think only "being itself," he is then quite aware of how extremely difficult this attempt is.

In the mid-1930s, Heidegger settled on a particular interpretation of "being." "Being" is, in truth, "the event of appropriation" (*das Ereignis*). In his first major work, Heidegger had already called attention to the interconnection between being and time. For Heidegger, the thought of the "event of appropriation" radicalizes this connection. This radicalization has more specifically to do with *one* determinate aspect of "temporality." For us, time happens as "history." In the notion of "event of appropriation," history becomes an important factor. It is also clear that this emphasis on history has an anchoring point in "factical life." It became more and more evident to Heidegger that the political events of his time did not fall from the sky. They came from their world; therefore, we can understand them by reflecting on their origin in European history.

Subsequently, in the second half of the 1930s, stimulated by an interpretation of Hölderlin's poetry that became ever more important for him, the philosopher is gripped by the thought that certain leitmotifs of European philosophy must be "overcome." Here, we must not overlook the coincidence of this goal with the ever more powerful and totalizing domination of the National Socialists. There is indeed a link between the "factical life" in the totalitarian State of the Third Reich (and all the horrors associated with it) and the notion of "overcoming metaphysics," a notion that goes back to the concept of "destructuring" (*Destruktion*) developed in the early 1920s. In this context, the question concerning technology and its power becomes an ever more burning one.

Right around this time, the aforementioned anti-Semitic affect erupts in Heidegger's thinking and gives rise to crude theses on Judaism. Here, Heidegger's contemporaneity with National Socialism acquires a terrifying ambivalence from which not even his interpretation of Hölderlin escapes unscathed. With the latter, the philosopher wishes to inscribe himself in an epochal destiny in which "the Greeks" and "the Germans" play the main roles. A "first inception" (with "the Greeks") is answered by "another inception" (with "the Germans"). As they abandon a world that has forgotten being, "the Germans" are charged with the mission of beginning history anew and in a completely different manner. According to Heidegger, Hitler's disastrous politics threatened to sabotage this mission. As this happened, Heidegger's thinking became ensnared in attacks against everything that encouraged this failure. Next to the military enemies of the German Reich, and the National Socialists who misinterpret "the German," we find "World-Judaism." The passages Heidegger dedicates to this subject are some of the most horrifying – but also the stupidest – passages the thinker ever wrote.

After the war, Heidegger uses two concepts to further develop the thinking of the "event of appropriation." In the 1930s, he had, in a very problematic way, characterized the "essence of technology" as "machination." He now understands it as "positionality" (*Ge-Stell*). "Positionality" corresponds to the concept of the "fourfold" (*Geviert*), which articulates the world in accordance with a fourfold structure. During this period, Heidegger occupies himself almost exclusively with the question of how the human being can live in an ever-increasingly technicized world. It thus becomes clear that, on the one hand, Heidegger did not believe that the fundamental ideas which determined his politics and ethics actually changed after 1945. On the other hand, in the discussion of "positionality," Heidegger overcomes a fatal one-sidedness in his understanding of "machination."

An introduction to Martin Heidegger's philosophy faces a particular problem of language. At first glance, Heidegger's conceptuality seems very simple. The philosopher hardly uses any technical terms. At times, he speaks an expressive but awkward German; at others, his German is plain and rough. In this manner, Heidegger makes use of everyday words but

in an entirely peculiar sense. This is already the case with
the words "life" or "event" (*Ereignis*). But if this is so, the
question of using quotation marks becomes a pressing one.
They will be rigorously used in the present text. When we
think about or with Heidegger, our thinking must remain free
from his thinking. It may neither let itself be seduced by the
power of his language nor simply appropriate his language
and concepts. In philosophy, it is essential that the reader
of philosophical texts remain free *both* when agreeing *and*
when disagreeing with them. This is not at all simple, but it
is essential nevertheless.

An introduction to Heidegger's thinking has to deal with
the problem that Heidegger's philosophy is an inexhaustible
source of new concepts. At times, Heidegger changes his terminology from lecture course to lecture course; he arrives at
new formulations from manuscript to manuscript. *One* meaning
can be expressed in a manifold way. These movements from
word to word have everything to do with the "path-like character" of Heideggerian thought. An introduction must follow
the rhythm of these inventions without being able to meet the
demand for completeness. I have tried from time to time to
offer the reader some help in this regard.

The present text is a *critical* introduction. In the truest sense
of the word, *krinō* means "to separate" (*scheiden*), "to divide,"
i.e., to make distinctions (*Unterscheidungen*) that result in a
decision (*Entscheidung*). However, the question stands: what
is our criterion? That is difficult to say. Presumably there is
more than one. It is certainly a matter of a universal reason
that is aware of its own weaknesses and dangers. Philosophy
must, however difficult it may be, hold fast to this criterion.
Over and beyond this, the criterion is above all "the other,"
particularly as attested in the poetry of Paul Celan.[14] Heidegger
faces the greatest problems when he annihilates and sacrifices
"the other" for the purposes of his narrative of "the history of
being." My criticism of Heidegger is in itself a plea for "the
other." It listens to the "silent voices" of the dead – of the
Shoah.[15] They listen very closely to us as we debate the events
of the twentieth century. They know what we will never know.
They are the origin of the conscience of our age. My view is
that it is above all *to them* that we owe the moral clarity in
matters regarding anti-Semitism and the Shoah.

This introduction is written for readers who are willing to put some effort into reading this book. Though philosophy asks questions that concern all human beings, it requires the free time and leisure of those who want to occupy themselves with it. This leisure does not preclude effort. Yet these efforts belong to the best possible activities we can undertake. For, in philosophy, we deal with ourselves, with our blind spots on which we try to shed some light. It is quite possible that this book will be particularly useful to philosophy students who encounter Heidegger. But it would be very nice if men and women who love philosophy also found the book stimulating.

In the *Gesamtausgabe* of Heidegger's works, 89 out of a planned total of 102 volumes have already appeared. Given this mass of texts, an introduction cannot possibly consider all the themes that Heidegger investigated. Therefore, I had to be selective and make certain decisions. Whoever does not find in this introduction this or that aspect of Heideggerian thought will hopefully be inspired by it to develop these ideas further on his or her own.

Nietzsche claimed that what is exemplary in a philosopher is his ability "to draw whole nations after him." "Indian history" in particular would give evidence of this. It is important that this philosophical example be "supplied by his outward life and not merely in his books." What matters for Nietzsche is how the philosopher "bears himself, what he wears and eats, his morals, and not so much what he says or writes." The philosopher must be seen; he must leave his writing desk and live. And Nietzsche concludes his meditation in a resigned manner: "How completely this courageous visibility of the philosophical life is lacking in Germany."[16]

Has Heidegger given us the "example" of a "philosophical life in Germany"? Or was it precisely such a life that he was denied by a Germany that subscribed to death with inexplicable energy? Or have he and his thinking only made this energy more powerful? It could perhaps be argued that German history of the twentieth century becomes visible in Heidegger's thought as in hardly any other thinker. Whoever wishes to become familiar with Heidegger's thinking has to come face to face, in an abyssal fashion, with the abysses of this history.

1

The "Facticity of Life"

"There was hardly more than a name, but the name traveled all over Germany like the rumor of the hidden king."[1]

Hannah Arendt

Phenomenology and hermeneutics

It is not easy to determine Martin Heidegger's philosophical beginning. At one point in a lecture course, he says: "Companions in my searching were the young Luther and the paragon Aristotle, whom Luther hated. Impulses were given by Kierkegaard, and Husserl opened my eyes."[2] Each of these figures left behind traces in Heidegger's thinking. However, it would be shortsighted to let this quartet suffice. Thus we would have to mention Wilhelm Dilthey and Oswald Spengler, or Hegel and Nietzsche, or Dostoyevsky and medieval philosophy. Heinrich Rickert, the neo-Kantian and Heidegger's teacher, writes in his comments on his student's qualifying dissertation (*Habilitationschrift*) that he could "achieve great success" in the study of the "spirit" of medieval logic.[3] In other words, Heidegger's philosophical starting point springs from many sources, and it would be a mistake to seek to derive his philosophizing from only one tradition.

In a journal entry from the 1940s, Heidegger mentions "in passing" the importance of his "*Habilitationschrift* on Duns Scotus' Doctrine of Categories and Signification."[4] The "Doctrine of Signification" and the "Doctrine of Categories" considered the "essence of language" and the "essence of being" respectively. "Right away" he had the "experience of the oblivion of being," and *Being and Time* was "on its way." This "journey" was "helped by Husserl's way of thinking." However, we can sense the intention to tell a story in such a retrospection. The beginning appears only belatedly, as it were. And yet Heidegger names what are arguably the two most important sources of his thinking.

It is possible to characterize the beginning of Heidegger's thought by means of two philosophical methods. These are two methodological decisions which the philosopher was already making in his first lecture courses and which repeatedly stimulated his philosophy with ever new impetuses. Early on, at the beginning of the 1920s, he immersed himself in the two philosophical methods and schools of "phenomenology" and "hermeneutics." "Schools" adequately names both of these ways of thinking only insofar as we learn in school *how* something can be thought. Thus we are not to understand phenomenology and hermeneutics as particular subject matters but, instead, as ways in which philosophical questions can be posed and answered.

Heidegger tells us that he worked on Edmund Husserl's *Logical Investigations* (1900) already as a student in his first semester in the winter of 1909–10. This work stands as the founding document of "phenomenology," a philosophical method aiming to investigate thematically not the theories of "things" but, instead, the "things themselves," the way and manner in which "things" are given to me, how they appear. In Greek, *phainomenon* means that which is appearing. "Phenomenology" is thus a way of thinking that concerns itself with what appears and its appearing.

Heidegger's first lecture courses already exhibit their own terminology and independence with respect to the thematic orientation of this method. The theme of these courses, the fundamental question of his thinking at that time, is "factical life." "Life" here means a mostly unthematized relation of the human being to himself. It is a form of "self-sufficiency."

I live on my own and in relation to myself. The "facticity of life," its factuality or givenness, consists in how existence and its motivations are fulfilled in the everyday. Life happens to us each time of its own accord, as it were. Heidegger expresses this by way of a turn of phrase: "Life is simply this way, thus it gives itself [*so gibt es sich*]."[5] A philosophy of "factical life" deals with these "modes of givenness." A phenomenon presents itself as a gift (*Phänomengabe*) that cannot be thought in advance.[6] Phenomenology is a restrained way of thinking because it contemplates what "there is" (*es gibt*).

Thus, in a way that is not entirely unproblematic, Heidegger does not allow biological or corporeal aspects to imbue the fundamental phenomenon of his early thinking, his concept of "life." Phenomenology is the "absolute original science *of spirit* in general."[7] It is therefore not the life of the body but rather the life of "spirit" that interests the theologically educated young philosopher. We can sense the influence of early readings of works by Georg Wilhelm Friedrich Hegel and Wilhelm Dilthey.[8] For example, in his *Phenomenology of Spirit*, Hegel had broken down the "life of spirit" into the metamorphoses proper to it.

Life is never present as an isolated object. It has each time its own place and its own time. "Our life is the world," writes Heidegger, meaning that life unfolds itself in a variety of ways into inscrutable relations to fellow human beings and things.[9] A phenomenology of life has to do with the "life-worlds" in which the human being is practically and theoretically caught up in his own manner.

The concept of "world" or "life-world" – already used by Husserl earlier on – corresponds especially to this concept of "life." It provides possibilities of a differentiation necessary to the full development of the concept of "life." Thus "world" is always "environing-world," "with-world" and "self-world."[10] We live in "worlds" that merge concentrically and that may eventually form a unified "world." I live with my friends, loved ones, and enemies, etc.; I live each time in a "personal rhythm." On the basis of such a differentiated understanding of "world," Heidegger carries out his phenomenological analysis. We shall see how, during the course of his thinking, Heidegger repeatedly investigates what he, in all seriousness, called the "problem of world."

The life Heidegger thematizes in his lecture courses at the beginning of the 1920s is a "factical" "existing." A fundamental uncertainty and finitude belong to "existence." There is a "life led astray," as well as a "genuine life."[11] The "life" that goes "astray" and the "genuine life" are not mutually exclusive. Both tendencies meet in the uncertainty of "life." "Life" has an aspect of "questionability" it cannot evade. The carrying out of "factical life" consists precisely in experiencing this "questionability" time and again. Life forms a "factical nexus of experience." "Experience" is the primary expression of "factical life" in the sense of being the access to it. This "experience" has nothing or only little to do with an empirical concept of experience. Heidegger's understanding of experience is always embedded in a particular pathos. One does not "have an experience"; one suffers it instead. It is always a pathetic "experience," a passive activity, as it were.

Already for the early Heidegger, a problem emerges out of these issues that will occupy him until the very end. If "experience" is the authentic access to the fundamental phenomenon of philosophy, if the philosopher can only speak about his topic if he "lives" this topic, then we have to pose the question of the "scientificity" of philosophy in general. Ordinarily, we assume philosophy to be a "science." Heidegger characterizes the latter as a "cognitive, rational comportment."[12] However, "life" consists only marginally in such a "comportment." For the most part, I experience "life" in a way that is precisely not "cognitive." This is why Heidegger calls attention early on to the fact that the "problem of the self-understanding of philosophy" was always "taken too lightly."[13]

If "life" is to be the theme of philosophy, and if the philosopher can only carry out this theme if he does not avoid "life," we can then infer that "philosophy arises from factical life experience."[14] For Heidegger, philosophy is from the beginning a finite activity of someone thinking – just as "life" is finite, so too is the thinking that thematizes this full life. The philosophy that "arises from factical life experience" "returns back into factical life experience."[15] This means that thinking is entangled in life, which makes it difficult to uphold the "ideal of science" for philosophy. At the same time, this makes it apparent that the divide between biography and thought – which Heidegger himself later argued for – can be called into question.

This initial insight into the entanglement of thought and life drove Heidegger early on to contemplate the relation between philosophy and the university. Already in the 1919 "war-emergency semester," Heidegger discusses the possibility of a "genuine reform in the university."[16,17] Three years later, he interrogates yet again the "life nexus" of the "university" and wonders "if the university should be further tailored towards needs."[18] When Heidegger broaches the "self-assertion of the German university" in 1933, he is harking back to a thematic complex that was dear to his heart already in the beginning of his philosophizing. If "life" is the beginning of philosophy, doesn't the "university" have to be its end?

"Facticity" is the term for the entanglement of thought and life. If Heidegger does not hold fast to this term throughout his career, we can nevertheless see that he remained faithful to the phenomenon of "facticity." In its finitude, philosophical thought is woven into the worldly entrapments of whoever might be philosophizing in a given moment, so that it cannot yield knowledge entirely extricated from these entrapments. Two essential instances of entanglement into facticity are the phenomena of "language" and "history."

Aristotle already characterized the human being as a living being that has language (*zōon logon echon*). Human life is distinguished by the fact that it is itself able to express things about itself. It is characteristic for human beings that "life always addresses itself and answers itself in its own language."[19] "Life" and "language" are not independent phenomena for the human but, instead, belong together from the outset. The emphasis of this co-belonging is indicative of an important tendency in Heidegger's thought. The life he has in view is the poetic or practical life I lead while working and dealing with others, the life in which I find myself in a constant conversation. Though Heidegger takes an interest precisely in the seemingly marginal zones of this conversation and of speech, i.e., "falling silent" or "silence," he remains skeptical about the supposedly non-linguistic instincts and drives of life.

A phenomenology of "life" has to do with the fact that this life expresses itself. Life happens within a range of significations and "significances." Our actions are target-specific; we pursue goals. I thus live "in the factical as in a wholly particular context of significances, which are continually permeating one another."[20] "Significances" refer to one another, contradict and intersect each other. When we contemplate life, we must turn to this constant occurrence of "significances."

On the one hand, the "significances" of "life" show themselves to the acting human being in "perception." As "appearances," they appear and form the object of "phenomenology." However, they call for being "interpreted." Factical action consists in a constant interpreting of disappearing and newly appearing aims and goals. This is why phenomenology is an interpretative encounter with what appears. Heidegger's phenomenology is a "phenomenological hermeneutics" from the start.[21]

Wilhelm Dilthey presumably prompted Heidegger's reference to "hermeneutics." However, the philosopher himself calls attention to the fact that the first explicit mention of hermeneutics names the god Hermes as its forefather.[22] Hermes is the messenger who communicates to men what the gods decide concerning them. Throughout the history of philosophy, hermeneutics became an art of interpreting texts. For instance, for Schleiermacher, hermeneutics is the art of "understanding" written messages. However, for Heidegger, this represents a reduction of the original concept of "hermeneutics." According to him, a life amidst significations is hermeneutical in general. "Factical life" is fundamentally an understanding – whether it has to understand and interpret itself or what happens in the world. Life is hermeneutical in itself because it is a life that questions, answers, understands, and misrecognizes itself.

Philosophy's contact with this life that understands and misunderstands itself is anything but a simple phenomenon. How does philosophy genuinely get a hold of "factical life?" We usually live in a fairly unreflective way in the everyday realm. We are immediately affected by what happens to us. Philosophy is, on the contrary, a mediating thinking; it is not only the reflection of our actions but, beyond that, the reflection of reflection. This situation shows itself in the way philosophy handles and deals with its objects, how it discusses

them. It is unable to remain simply in the "factical." It gives
life's problems "an objectivity" that factical phenomena do
not typically have; it makes life's phenomena into objects they
were not in their daily existence. There is a difference between
a philosophical treatment of love or death and the life in
which love and death affect us. This "formal determination
of the objective" in philosophy is for Heidegger a "prejudice,"
a pre-given attitude which also determines the conceptuality
of philosophizing.[23] A "phenomenological hermeneutics of
facticity" must take this pre-given attitude into account.

According to Heidegger, so-called "formal indication"
accomplishes this. It is a hermeneutical method that lets the
"factical" remain "undecided," that "formally" points to it
without measuring it up to a preexisting philosophical conceptuality so as to lose its immediate and clear meaning. "Formal
indication" has, for the "hermeneutics of facticity," an "indis-
pensable meaning" because it limits the validity claims of
philosophical conceptual orders.[24] "Formal indication" attempts
to let the "factical" appear in philosophy such as it is.

The "significances" we understand and interpret in life
form a given temporal nexus. I do not simply live in the today
but I deal with meanings that previous generations pass onto
me or that are still coming toward me from the future. "Factical life" is a life in history. The early Heidegger characterized
this phenomenon as the "historical."[25] He goes as far as to
argue that the concept of the "factical" becomes intelligible
only in terms of the "concept of the historical." For history
always determines the "factical" of our lives in one way or
another. Thus only if we take the Shoah into consideration
do we understand certain premises of political public life in
the Federal Republic of Germany.

In tandem with this phenomenon, we may not merely conceive of "history" as the object of historiography. In historiography, the "historical" is no longer understood in terms
of the "facticity of life" but becomes, instead, objectified as
an object to be researched. Heidegger concerns himself with
the "immediate vivacity" of the "historical" or, as he vividly
says, the "living historicality, which, as it were, has eaten its
way into our existence."[26] This "living historicality" imparts
itself to us chiefly by way of tradition. A "living historicality"
is a cultural heritage we can objectify in historiography but

in which we (and this also means historians) primarily "live." The foundations of European culture in Greek philosophy, Roman jurisprudence, and Christian religion form a "living historicality." We can find their traces everywhere in "factical life." To give an example, let us once more refer to the Shoah. On the one hand, it has an influence on our everyday life but it can, on the other hand, be made into an object of historiography.

For Heidegger, the "immediate vivacity" of history has a priority over its objectification in science. This priority flows from the fact that "factical life" itself should constantly provide a reference point to which history remains tied. History is for him a history lived in the here and now. When we make it into a purely theoretical object, we miss its genuine sense. Later, this thought that history is an intensely lived history will unleash an often unbridled rage toward historiography since the latter has, according to Heidegger, lost contact with the "living historicality" and the "history of being." "Historiography" is then nothing other than the technology that ruins everything.[27]

Heidegger's early turn to history flows systematically from the notion of a "phenomenological hermeneutics of facticity." "Factical life" is historically constituted in itself. I have shown how certain methodological problems arose from this determination of philosophy. First, a tension emerges in the relation between philosophy and science. Scientificity, as defined by Max Weber, for instance, consists in an unbiased freedom of perspectives we never adopt or even strive for in "factical life." What is at stake in the latter are, precisely, practical aims and goals, accomplishments of ethical orientations and biases. Secondly, a tension arises between the "hermeneutics of facticity" and the traditional conceptual structures of philosophy itself. This tension announces itself in Heidegger's notions of "formal indication" and of a specifically hermeneutical mode of access to the "factical." Both problems are centered on the meaning of the "living historicality" of thought. They stem from its ancient tradition. The questions "How does philosophy relate to an established ideal of scientificity?" and "Is philosophy able to get a hold of 'factical life' by means of its own traditions?" show that it is necessary to submit the history of European thought itself to a "destructuring"

(*Destruktion*). This is introduced as a "fundamental part of phenomenological philosophizing."[28]

The word *Destruktion* stems from the Latin word *destruere* (to destroy). The "phenomenological *Destruktion*" of the European history of thought does not aim, however, simply to destroy traditional scientific and philosophical thought. It should, rather, shake up this tradition so as to undo concealments and distortions of the sources of this tradition. There is a tendency in Heidegger's thinking from the outset to lay bare the "origins" of "factical life," along with the thinking that comes from and goes back to these sources. The first characterization of phenomenology as a "science of origins" already bears witness to this intention.

Part of what is peculiar to Heidegger is that, for him, the provenance of European "facticity" or, if you like, identity springs from two sources. The "hermeneutics of facticity" has to do with a "Greco-Christian interpretation of life."[29] Initially, Heidegger pays no attention to the traditional roots of Roman Antiquity that he will deal with polemically later on. The *Destruktion* of the European history of thought relates to both of these two sources accordingly, namely, Christian theology and western philosophy. Thus he writes during the winter semester course of 1920–1, "It cannot be avoided that the discovery of the phenomenal complexes changes from the ground up the problematic and the formation of concepts and offers authentic measures for the destructuring [*Destruktion*] of Christian theology and western philosophy."[30]

At the outset of his thinking, Heidegger describes the thematic that was to occupy him his entire life. It is a matter of dismantling or laying bare the sources of "factical life," of a life that seeks to understand itself and, as a result, contemplates its history.

The "primordial Christian facticity of life"

In a short text from 1954, Heidegger recalls his childhood:

> On Christmas morning at around half past three, the bell-ringer's boys [*Läutenbuben*] came to the sexton-home [*Mesmerhaus*]. There, the sexton-mother [*Mesmermutter*] had covered the table with cake, coffee and milk for them. The

table stood next to the Christmas tree whose scent of fir and candles from Christmas Eve still lingered in the warm living room. For weeks, if not the whole year, the bell-ringer's boys looked forward to these hours in the sexton-home. Where may the magic of these hours have concealed itself?[31]

Heidegger's father was the "sexton" or "sacristan" of the Catholic church of St Martin by the castle in Meßkirch, the philosopher's birthplace. The "bell-ringer's boys" showed up to help with the seven-part bell ringing (famous nationwide, we can listen to it on the internet) and to resound the *mystery of the belfry tower*. The Catholic theologian Conrad Gröber, also born in Meßkirch and archbishop of Freiburg starting in 1932, belonged to those who first encouraged the adolescent thinker. It was natural for Heidegger to begin studying theology in Freiburg in 1909–10. Much later, again in 1954, Heidegger wrote, "Without this theological past I should never have come upon the path of thinking. But the past (*Herkunft*) always remains the future (*Zukunft*)."[32] Heidegger's philosophical beginning is tied to that "magic" of the "scent of fir and candles."

If one finds hardly any traces of a systematic confrontation with theology or Christianity in Heidegger's mature thinking, at the beginning of his years as lecturer this is not the case. The phenomenological-hermeneutical study of the "facticity of life" spontaneously led to the phenomenon of "history." The philosopher must submit the latter to a *Destruktion*, to an uncovering of the original thoughts which lasting and sedimented interpretations have buried in the course of history. As part of this hermeneutical turn to history, Heidegger writes in the summer semester of 1920, "There is the necessity of a fundamental confrontation with Greek philosophy and its disfiguration of Christian existence. *The true idea of Christian philosophy*; Christian not a label for a bad and epigonal Greek philosophy. The way to a primordial Christian – Greek-free – theology."[33]

The genuine kernel of Christianity is "Christian existence," a concept with an unmistakable Kierkegaardian influence. This existence undergoes a "disfigurement" by means of "Greek philosophy," which we are to set aside by way of a *Destruktion*. We can examine the *"true idea of Christian philosophy"* solely on the basis of such a *Destruktion*.

The motif of the reference to "Christian existence" flows from a phenomenological-hermeneutical study of "factical life." The latter shows up as entangled in "historical connections." The goal to "gain a real and original relationship to history" is conducive to Heidegger's clarification of "facticity." Heidegger outlines this goal with the methodological knowledge that "history exists only from out of a present." If these guidelines prompt a reference to Christian existence, the latter is then tied to both the question of "history" and the "present," on the basis of which this question is to be formulated and to which it always remains bound.[34]

The relation to history does not only concern the methodological problem that each conception of the "meaning of history" is dependent upon the point of view of whoever wishes to conceive this meaning. The fact that the present is linked to the "meaning of history" points to the relation between "history" and "time": life in history is a temporal phenomenon in itself. This becomes immediately apparent because history contains dates and facts that are bygone. These, however, do not have a significance merely as bygone. To the extent that I concern myself with history from out of the present, history has a significance for "factical life" in the here and now.

The question of history thus introduces the problem of the "temporality" of "factical life." The phenomenological way of thinking requires that the relation between "historicality" and "temporality" should be explicated in the "original factical experience of temporality" itself. Heidegger studies this "factical experience" of "temporality" with a view to "primordial Christian religiosity."[35] For him, this "primordial Christian religiosity" is the "factical life experience" itself: "Factical life experience is historical. Christian religiosity lives temporality as such."[36]

In order to make these connections clear, Heidegger carries out an interpretation of two Letters to the Thessalonians (both of which he ascribes to Paul) contained in the New Testament. On the basis of this interpretation, Heidegger extracts the fundamental traits of a "primordial Christian religiosity," i.e., of a "Christian existence."

The "aim" of "primordial Christian religiosity" is "salvation" (*sōtēria*) and "life" (*zōē*). The "fundamental comportment of Christian consciousness" is to be understood in terms of these two poles. We may glean the Christian relation to salvation – and to the life that springs from this relation – solely from a specific situation of existence: salvation is "announced" and with it goes the injunction to abandon the everyday life marked by pre-Christian habits. In "primordial Christian existence," we are dealing with a "complete break with the earlier past, with every non-Christian view of life."[37] This "complete break" concerns the past of a particular existence. It consists at the same time in an "absolute turning-around."[38] The issue is not simply to abandon what once used to be a habit but to turn oneself to another mode of existence to the extent that one inherits and accomplishes the latter as a possibility of life.

Christian life acquires a most peculiar characteristic with this "complete break." The "absolute turning-around" (*metanoia*) as a "break" is not to be understood in the manner of a gradual change. Something immediately stops in the "break"; something else starts. Christian life begins only when one carries out this "break." This is not to say that the will of an acting subject governs the life that was started otherwise. The "facticity" of Christian life "cannot be won out of one's own strength"; it "originates from God."[39] Christian existence is conscious of the fact that it springs from God's "grace." To be a Christian is not an original possibility for humans. Christian existence is a "grace" of God, meant to be received only by means of that break which terminates a bygone age and discloses a new present.

For the "primordial Christian facticity," this turn to a new present goes together with the fact that Jesus Christ announced his return, which would thus bring all ages to an end (in theology, we speak of "Parousia expectation" and "eschatology," of an awaited new presence of Christ which will end time and consequently history). A peculiar tension thereby emerges in the present which has repercussions not only for the future but also for life in the here and now. We do not attain "salvation" solely in terms of the present. It comes to us from the future above all. The life that awaits the "Second Coming" thus finds itself presently in "distress." Everything we do and must do in the present stands under the sign of this "Coming." The Christian is "living incessantly in the only-yet, which intensifies his distress."[40] What must be done is "yet" to be done. The "Christian existence" which has, in a complete break, left the bygone non-Christian life behind cannot evade "distress." It must remain open to the "Second Coming" by means of an "entering-oneself-into-anguish."[41] The "factical experience" of time and history thus consists in such an "anguish" with respect to a futural fulfillment of existence.

This type of "compressed temporality" does not allow us to determine or inquire more precisely into the moment of the Lord's return. The "factical experience" of this temporality is without its "own order and demarcations."[42] It is neither an objective nor a subjective experience of time. We may not await the "Second Coming" as a "special event that is futurally situated in temporality."[43] Christian existence consists solely in an immediate suffering of an "anguish" that emanates from the heralded "salvation" so as to promise "redemption."

A particular "factical experience" intensifies this "anguish." The author of the *Second Letter to the Thessalonians* speaks of a certain condition for Christ's return. Before the Lord appears, an "adversary" (*Second Letter to the Thessalonians* I, 4) must emerge. This "adversary" is characterized as "Satan" (I, 9). It is perhaps characteristic of Heidegger that he takes this matter particularly seriously. For, he concludes, "whether one is a true Christian is decided by the fact that one recognizes the Antichrist."[44] The particular temporal experience of "Christian existence" implies knowledge of what is "against God."[45] This knowledge consists in seeing through the lies and temptations spread by the Antichrist. We cannot reach "salvation" without the possibility or danger of getting lost in the temptations of what is "against God." The presence of the Antichrist decisively determines the present "distress" of "Christian existence."

"Christian existence," which "lives" "temporality as such," is familiar with "what is against God" – which primarily presents itself neither as original sin nor as moral fault, but rather as "Satan's" real figure (the mythical incarnation of evil). In a letter from 1921, Heidegger writes to his teacher Rickert, "In phenomenology, research on conscience has become unavoidable." This remark is certainly made in the context of a philosophy of religion. "Research on conscience" becomes necessary in "Christian existence" because "what is against

God" emerges in the "factical experience" of temporality. Later, Heidegger will at one point say that "evil" "does not consist in the mere baseness of human action but rather in the malice of rage."[46] The latter belongs to "being itself." Fully in accordance with his early interpretation of the *Letter to the Thessalonians*, "evil" or "what is evil-like" is thus not the subjective property of the human being but rather happens in a historico-temporal way.

At this point, in light of the anti-Semitism of the *Black Notebooks*, it is impossible not to ask to what extent we can already detect anti-Semitic or anti-Jewish tendencies in Heidegger's reflections on the phenomenology of religion. For example, Heidegger remarks that "the original Greek text is the only one to be used as a basis" for his research.[47] It has been noticed that, in this way, Heidegger dissimulates the extent to which Hebrew deeply influences Paul's Greek text.[48] Moreover, the radicality of the "complete break" with the past that "Christian existence" requires is not far from the thought that Judaism, i.e., the Old Testament, is one of the things that we should leave behind. Indeed, Heidegger remarks that Paul "is struggling with the Jews and the Jewish Christians," that is to say, the Jews who converted to Christianity.[49] And is the experience of time which Heidegger ascribes to Christianity not dependent on a Jewish messianism that the philosopher overlooks?[50] This is entirely possible and it may lead us to conclude that Heidegger repressed the significance of Judaism. He certainly elided it with his interest in the "Greco-Christian interpretation of life." Later anti-Semitic statements allow us to infer retrospectively that this oversight is not at all accidental. Yet would we have asked ourselves if Heidegger's interpretation of St Paul is anti-Semitic had we not known about the later statements about Judaism? In this instance – and, as we shall see, in others – we run up against the dilemma that an anti-Semitism is here merely being hinted at without being unequivocally attested. We run up against the hermeneutical problem of "suspicion" that I will delve into later.

Heidegger's phenomenologico-hermeneutical treatment of the Christian tradition of faith is under the sign of an elabora-tion of "primordial-Christian-factical existence," of primordial Christianity. His goal stems from the program of the "phe-nomenological destructuring" of history. The attempt to enable

an original understanding of "factical life" – and of its entanglement in time and history – lies at the center of this project.
Heidegger's interpretation of "Christian existence" takes place
over the course of a short period in the beginning of the 1920s.
He never came back to it in this form. This, of course, does
not allow us to underestimate the value that these analyses
have for Heidegger's thinking. It is thus clear that it is a
Christian (Jewish-messianic) understanding of time, rather
than a Greek one, that determines Heidegger's own notion of
temporality. The most important characteristic of this notion
of time consists both in the priority of the future vis-à-vis the
past and the present, and in the special significance that this
relation to the future has for actual praxis, which is radically
modified by this future. It must be pointed out, however, that
toward the end of World War II Heidegger arrived at the
notion of an "eschatology of being" and thereby attempted
to incorporate the Christian notion of time into the "history
of being."[51]

Inceptions: Plato and Aristotle

Heidegger's point of departure is that we can only gain knowledge of life's "facticity" if we interpret its historical origin. It
is the "Greco-Christian interpretation of life" that constitutes
the historical origin of "our" "facticity" (we have already
made reference to Heidegger's deliberate repression of any
Jewish influences). A "hermeneutics of facticity" must give
an account of how this "interpretation of life" determines its
conceptuality and practical significance.

A Christian interpretation of Greek sources is at the root of
certain things taken for granted about the human being that
seem to go without saying and that determine the European
concept of humanity. For Heidegger, the point of departure
of such an interpretation is Plato's and Aristotle's philosophy. A specific retroactive transference of Christian-theological
categories into Aristotelian philosophy has given rise to the
Christian notion of the human being, especially during the
scholastic theology of the Middle Ages, a discipline which
Heidegger knew well due to his study of Catholic theology. For
Heidegger, then, it was only natural to refer his elaboration of

the "facticity of life" back to a more original interpretation of Aristotelian philosophy. The latter is supposed to go behind the Christian-Scholastic appropriation of Aristotle. The earliest evidence of this regression is a 1922 text that Heidegger prepared for the philosopher Paul Natorp at the latter's request in order to establish a solid basis for the faculty position which had opened up at Marburg University, a position which Heidegger obtained. The so-called "Natorp Report" summarized the results Heidegger had just communicated in his lecture courses over the course of those early years. In addition, the report makes up the core of the book *Being and Time: Part One*, which was published five years later. The report is a phenomenological elaboration of Aristotelian texts.

Above all, the uniqueness of Heidegger's approach to Aristotle's philosophy consists in interpreting the texts of the great co-originator of European philosophy as a conceptual unfolding of practical-poietic life – poietic in the sense of manufacturing or producing. The displacement of the concept of life is decisive here. Life is now grasped as "being," that is to say, "life" is "ontologically" understood. As Heidegger says during a lecture course from this period: "At issue is being, i.e., that it 'is,' the *meaning of being*, that being 'is,' i.e., is there as being genuinely and according to its import (in the phenomenon)."[52] In this context, Heidegger characterizes life as "human Dasein," i.e., a particular "being": "life = existence, 'being' in and through life."[53] The object of philosophical thinking is the "being-like character" of "human Dasein." Hermeneutical phenomenology becomes "*ontological* phenomenology."[54] In this way, Heidegger sets up the basic framework for the conceptuality of *Being and Time*.

This displacement of the concept of "life" into the question of "being" is a decisive step of Heidegger's thinking in general. The "question of the meaning of being," as Heidegger calls it in *Being and Time*, animated and troubled Heidegger's thinking time and again. It is the axis and pivotal point of all his idiosyncratic paths. I will come back to this.

The reinterpretation of "life" as "being" can be traced back to the way in which Aristotelian philosophy acted as a stimulus for Heidegger. Aristotle develops his ontology in his lectures on nature, i.e., physics (*phusis* = nature), and on the being which goes beyond nature and forms its backdrop (the being *meta ta phusika*, i.e., the being "behind" natural things; there is another editorial sense to the concept of "metaphysics" that I am skipping over here). In the beginning of the fourth Book of *The Metaphysics* (1003 a21), Aristotle talks about a science (*epistēmē*) that contemplates "being as being" (*to on hē on*). This theory of "being" (*Sein*) is incommensurable with any other science because these other sciences investigate particular "beings" (*Seiende*) – for example, a particular being such as a number – and do not deal with "being as being" in general.[55] Given that philosophy is an investigation and questioning of the first causes (*aitiai* or *archai*) of "beings," a theory of "being" as such would have to search for its first causes.

This particular theory of "being as such" distinguishes Aristotle's thought from the other sciences. Not every form of knowledge deals with the first foundations of "beings." Thus, next to theoretical knowledge (*epistēmē theoretikē*), we find a knowledge of the political (*epistēmē politikē*), of action (*epistēmē praktikē*), and of production (*epistēmē poietikē*). Theoretical knowledge encompasses three regions of "beings": natural things (physics); numbers (mathematics); and the divine (theology). These theoretical sciences have precedence over the other types of science; and among them, the science of the divine stands out. Therefore, the theory that contemplates the divine is first philosophy pure and simple (*prōtē philosophia*, 1026 a24).

In the first instance, to investigate "beings" means to deal with the essence (*ousia*) of "beings." Aristotle determines this essence in a threefold manner (1069 a30). The senses perceive two natural (moved) essences that differ from a third (unmoved) essence. As for the two natural essences, the first is every living being that perishes, the second the eternal stars. The unmoved essence is the divine (*theion*) or God (*theos*). According to Aristotle, this God is sheer Spirit, i.e., thought (*nous*). It is pure actuality (*energeia*): it fulfills the best of all activities insofar as it can keep thinking without end. Since it can only think the best, it constantly thinks itself. Thus Aristotle is able to characterize this essence as thought thinking itself (*noēsis noēseōs*, 1074 b24). This divine essence is supposed to have set the whole of "beings" in motion. It is the essence that moves everything without being itself moved (*ti kinoun auto akinēton*). This essence is the unmoved prime mover (*prōton kinoun akinēton*).

For Aristotle, human happiness consists in the contemplation of the divine. This contemplation is not a practical or poietic activity but is, rather, theoretical. By subscribing to theory or first philosophy as theology, Aristotle oriented European philosophy and Christian theology in a manner that still determines the ethos and pathos of many philosophers today.

Heidegger was nevertheless against Aristotle's decision. Heidegger's concrete interpretation of Aristotle's texts centers around Book VI of the *Nicomachean Ethics*. It is in this text that Aristotle discusses the so-called "dianoetic virtues," that is, the virtues or "excellences" (derived from the Greek word *aretē*) that guide thought and knowledge. Heidegger emphasizes two of these virtues: practical wisdom (*phronēsis*) and theoretical wisdom (*sophia*).

According to Heidegger, *phronēsis* is the "circumspective care" for the practical relevance of everyday life.[56] It guides our dealings with everyday issues without asking ultimate and final questions. *Phronēsis* is a helpful knowledge to have when dealing with the events of everyday life; it is a kind of worldly wisdom (*Lebensklugheit*). *Phronēsis* does not know an ultimate truth of theoretical wisdom but rather a truth that has practical significance. "Practical truth" is "nothing other than the whole unveiled moment (at the particular time) of factical life in the how of its decisive readiness for dealings with itself."[57] This "whole unveiled moment of factical life" encompasses our entire field of action that does not ultimately come down to epistemological judgments. Heidegger began his deep engagement with Aristotle's thought at a time when he was especially committed to the phenomenon of "factical life." Thus we understand why it is that Heidegger considered the dianoetic *aretē* of *phronēsis* to be a decisive Aristotelian discovery.

By contrast, *sophia* entails something else for Heidegger. It is an "authentic understanding that consists in looking at something," that is to say, it reaches its highest fulfillment in the contemplation of "the idea of the divine."[58] Unlike *phronēsis*, which is expert at "practical truth," *sophia* has knowledge of the highest theoretical truth. The latter is the divine which, for Aristotle, is accessible "not by means of a fundamental religious experience" but "by a radicalization of the idea of beings that are moved." According to Heidegger, this "being-moved" consists in a "pure perceiving," that is, "it must be free of *any emotional relation* to its towards-which." Regardless of whether or not this interpretation is accurate, what is at stake here for Heidegger are "the basic ontological structures that later decisively influenced the notion of divine being in the specific Christian sense." Here, Heidegger wants to call attention to the fact that, insofar as Christian theology – and the philosophical speculations it influenced, such as German idealism – go back to Aristotle's first philosophy, they speak in "*foreign categories that are foreign to their own domain of being.*" In contrast to this mixture of philosophical and Christian concepts, Heidegger emphasizes a clear difference between Greek ontology and Christian preaching. I have already shown how Heidegger's interpretation of the Pauline texts of primordial Christianity does not become ensnared in the "basic ontological structures" that were introduced into Christian theology by – but *not only* by – the medieval reception of Aristotle.

By differentiating between Greek philosophy and Christian religion, Heidegger attempted to find a foundation for his own thought, a goal that guided his engagement with Aristotle's philosophy. Heidegger believed that the course of European thinking had produced a confusion of traditions in which the original knowledge of what philosophy is – of what it means to be a philosopher – had been lost. Heidegger thought that he could work out this knowledge by going back to Greek philosophy. This was something he attempted, however, not just in his interpretations of Aristotle but also in his lectures on Plato.

The 1924–5 winter semester lecture course on *The Sophist* shows how close Heidegger is to Plato's philosophy. Initially, Heidegger proposes to return to Plato's thought via Aristotle. He adheres to the following hermeneutical principle: "interpretation should proceed from the clear into the obscure."[59] This return to Plato is supposed to lead us more deeply into the origin of European philosophy. Heidegger seeks to learn from Plato what philosophy originally means, i.e., what it means to be a philosopher.

For it is the dialogue that discusses what it means to be a philosopher, as opposed to a sophist, that fulfills "the task of clarifying what the philosopher is."[60] However, Heidegger does not merely wish to communicate this distinction to his students but, rather, to unfold it step by step by means of an interpretation of the dialogue. In Plato, we are dealing with a "presentation of the issues" that explicitly tells us what it means to be a sophist. The dialogue thus becomes a "test" of whether or not the philosophy of the twentieth century can have "the freedom of substantive research."[61] The meditation on Greek philosophy is supposed to demonstrate whether contemporary thinking can still muster the necessary energy to be "philosophy."

It is, then, clearly impossible to shed light on the essence of the philosopher without asking about the subject matter of philosophy. Heidegger's interest in this dialogue lies especially in the passages where Plato investigates this issue. In this sense, the following passage from Plato is extremely important. Later on, Heidegger turned this passage into a kind of epigraph of *Being and Time*: "So since we're quite puzzled about it all, it's for you to clarify for us what exactly you intend to indicate when you utter the word 'being.' Clearly you've known all along; we used to think we did, but now find ourselves puzzled" (244a).[62] "The central and real concern [...] of the whole dialogue" is to find an answer to the question concerning the sense, or the senses, of "being."[63]

A little later in the dialogue, the "stranger" (*xenos*), the main character of *The Sophist*, describes the analysis of the signification of "being" as a *gigantomachia peri tēs ousias* (a battle of giants over "being"). Accordingly, Heidegger asks himself what the "stranger" really means by this reference to a philosophical battle over "being." What is at stake in this enigmatic description? For Heidegger, *"the issue is the disclosure of the being which genuinely satisfies the meaning of being."*[64] This is an insight which holds sway not only over one of the major works of twentieth-century philosophy but also, and beyond that, over Heidegger's entire thinking: to philosophize means to pose the question of "the meaning of being." European philosophy as a whole would fundamentally be nothing less than the project to pose and answer this question, each time in a different way.

What is important to see in all of this is that, since Plato, European philosophy had *never explicitly posed* the question of the "meaning of being." Even Plato himself, the great master of European thinking, did not formulate this question. However, this does not mean that Plato or Aristotle were not familiar with the "meaning of being." On the contrary, the reason why Plato and Aristotle did not pose the question of the meaning of being is because this meaning was too "obvious" for them. From here onward, the "meaning of being" forms something like the unthematized backdrop of Greek – and thus European – philosophizing. With Heidegger, a "subsequent interpretation" is supposed to make "this uninterrogated self-evident fact" explicit. Heidegger's philosophy understands itself as this "subsequent interpretation." However, here one must consider the extent to which the philosopher's interpretation modifies and reinterprets the "meaning of being" in a way that liberates him from the immediate influences of the Platonico-Aristotelian beginning of European philosophy.

In a concise manner, Heidegger raises this "obvious" "meaning of being," which surreptitiously guided Plato's and Aristotle's thought, to the level of the concept. As he puts it in a nutshell: "being = presence [*Anwesenheit*]."[65] Heidegger comes to this knowledge by referring to a specific sense of the Greek word *ousia*. In Greek, *ousia* does not simply mean "being" or "essence" (*Wesen*). Just as the German word *Anwesen* also means "property" or "house," *ousia* also means *Anwesen* in this sense of "property." When someone refers to his "property," his grounds and land, he means something on which he can rely. His property does not first have to come into being nor is it something bygone. It is present (*anwesend*) to him. For Heidegger, this connection between *ousia* and *Anwesen* indicates that the "meaning of being" must have something to do with *time*.

The "meaning of being" as "presence" does not emerge out of a particular philosophical idea. Rather, it emerges out of "factical life," as the sense of *ousia* as *Anwesen* (in the sense of property or house) demonstrates. According to Heidegger, neither Plato nor Aristotle, nor the philosophers who came after them, ever considered the "meaning of being," which thus remained unthematized. However, this meaning is the gravitational center of European philosophy because "it includes the whole problem of time and consequently the problem of the ontology of Dasein."[66] It thus became necessary for Heidegger to explicitly make the question of the "meaning of being" into the essential task of philosophy.

By displacing the theme of the "facticity of life" into the "meaning of being," Heidegger's thought arrives at one of its most important paths. According to Heidegger, to philosophize simply means to follow the Greek legacy whose beginning, however, predates Plato. This is why Heidegger returns time and again not only to Plato and Aristotle, but also to those he deemed to be "more incipient" (*anfänglichere*), i.e., the pre-Socratic thinkers who were close to the Greek poetry of Homer, Pindar, and Sophocles. This emphasis on the importance of the Greek coinage of the European philosophical tradition was unquestionably something that mobilized twentieth-century philosophy. Neither Husserl's phenomenology nor Ernst Cassirer's neo-Kantianism had any special relation to the Greek inception (*Anfang*) of philosophy. Hannah Arendt once expressed this in the following manner:

> It was technically decisive that we did not simply talk *about* Plato and expound his theory of Ideas. Rather, for an entire semester a single dialogue was pursued and subjected to question step-by-step, until the time-honored doctrine had disappeared to make room for a set of problems of immediate and urgent relevance. Today this sounds quite familiar, because nowadays many proceed in this way; but no one did before Heidegger.[67]

Heidegger's constant recourse to "the Greeks," his ability to let their thinking shine forth in a vital manner, has influenced generations of philosophers and philologists – who have also, of course, been very critical of Heidegger. There can be no doubt that this has given rise to a systematic increase in our ability to interpret major events of the twentieth century in a deeper way. It must be noted, however, that Heidegger was resolved in his decision to favor the Greek tradition of thinking; for him, to philosophize always means to question "being" (*Sein*).

Decades later, Heidegger at one point remarked that, were he ever "to write a theology," "the word 'being' [*Sein*] would not occur in it."[68] In his interpretation of the "factical life" of primordial Christianity, Heidegger had a phenomenon in mind which the "basic ontological structures" of Platonic-Aristotelian thinking were unable to grasp. The step from "factical life" to "factical Dasein," from the "facticity of life" to the "meaning of being," does not appear to have been a necessary one. Thus there are some Heidegger scholars who are interested precisely in these early lecture courses on the "facticity of life."[69] However, even if the movement from the "facticity of life" to the "meaning of being" is not at all a necessary one, Heidegger did not neglect to reflect further on the phenomenon of "facticity" in *Being and Time*. Here, this phenomenon is an aspect of "fundamental ontology."

2

The "Meaning of Being"

The analytic of Dasein or existence as "being-toward-death"

By the time *Being and Time: Part One* appeared in 1927, Heidegger had not published anything in eleven years. The book changed the premises of the debates first in German philosophy and then in European philosophy as a whole. It is considered today to be one of the most important philosophical works of the twentieth century. Even Jürgen Habermas, one of Heidegger's fiercest critics, noted the following regarding the publication of *Being and Time*: "Even from today's standpoint, Heidegger's new beginning probably presents the most profound turning point in German philosophy since Hegel."[1] *Being and Time* fundamentally influenced philosophers such as Jean-Paul Sartre and Emmanuel Levinas. But it was not only in philosophy that the influence of the book was felt: the psychoanalyst Jacques Lacan also found it compelling. In addition, the work also provoked responses from theological and literary circles alike.

With *Being and Time*, the thinker Heidegger appears on the big stage of philosophy. We will not understand the book's enormous historical consequences if we only consider the theoretical revolutions that happen in it. Its success is no doubt related to its style. Here, we are dealing with a distinctive writing style that charms just as much as it puts off the reader. For example, the Germanist Emil Staiger speaks of the "obscure power of Heidegger's language," which captivated him in an "irresistible" manner when he read *Being and Time* for the first time. As Staiger says, the "general public tends to be very critical" of Heidegger's use of language. Yet Staiger admits that, for him, "Heidegger's language is one of the greatest accomplishments of philosophical prose."[2] No matter how a reader experiences and evaluates Heidegger's style – not to mention the way in which the relationship between philosophy and style is understood – it is indeed the case that Heidegger's texts, like those of Hegel or Nietzsche, are written in a prose style that makes distinctive use of the German language.

Being and Time is an unfinished book manuscript. The first six editions bear the subtitle *Part One*. On the basis of the "outline of the treatise" in §8, we see that Heidegger did not even finish the first of the two parts he had planned. That being said, "The Basic Problems of Phenomenology" – a lecture course Heidegger gave in Marburg during the summer of 1927 – contains the revised third division that Heidegger had envisioned for the conclusion of the first part. The question of whether Heidegger had already written sections of the unpublished second part and then destroyed them because they were philosophically unsatisfactory is a legendary one. According to all the evidence that we have regarding this issue, we must in fact assume that a continuation of *Being and Time* was held back. This casts a special light on the "path-like character" of Heidegger's thinking. Even the text that could most plausibly be characterized as a "work" is but a fragmentary trace of Heidegger's thinking from sometime between 1920 and 1926.

In *Being and Time*, Heidegger again picks up the thread he had begun to weave in the "Natorp Report" and in his lecture course on Plato's *Sophist*. He poses the question of the "meaning of being," seeking to put this question on a "foundation": the philosopher thus calls the project of *Being and Time* "fundamental ontology." He chooses an "exemplary being" as the point of departure for his attempt to answer the question of the "meaning of being."[3] This "being" "is concerned, in its being, *about* its very being," that is to say, it is a "being" who can concern itself not just with itself but with "being itself" (*Sein selbst*). Insofar as it "always already" possesses an "understanding of being," this "being" is different from all other beings. This "being" is the human being. The human "understands" and is thus able to question "being" (*Sein*). Yet Heidegger gives this particular "being" (*Seiendes*) a name or terminological term of its own. The "being" who can question "being" is Dasein, i.e., the human being.

There is something peculiar about this designation, which other philosophers such as Kant or Hegel had already used, albeit in a different sense. The statement that the human being – the "essence" of the human, i.e., what makes him human – is Dasein precisely to the extent that he "understands being," this statement does not preclude the human "essence" from being characterized otherwise. In Plato, the human is the living being who can dance because he knows what rhythm is (*Laws*, 653 e). In Aristotle, the human is the political being because he has language – *zōon politikon*, i.e., *zōon logon echon* (*Politics*, 1253 a). In Christianity, as the image of God (*imago dei*), the human is conceived as the creature (*ens creatum*) of the creator (*ens increatum*). We could add other definitions of the human or humanity to this series. This gives off an impression of arbitrariness that Heidegger seeks to overcome by means of his essential and "ontologico-fundamental" determination, that is to say, Dasein.

In *Being and Time*, we do not find the formulation "the human being is Dasein"; rather, it is said that "Dasein is the human being." It is not as if the generic term "human being" functioned as the common root of different definitions, one of which would be Dasein. Nor is Dasein a human property for Heidegger. Rather, Dasein is the ground on the basis of which the human, who precisely "is," begins to be. To the extent that Dasein is this foundation, the human can be determined either as a dancing or political living being. Having said this, for Heidegger the human being can also be Dasein or "*Da-sein*" – and nothing else besides.

Dasein is not a property of the object "human being." For Heidegger, Dasein is the "being of the there."[4] We may not understand this "there" in the deictic sense of pointing, as in "a man is over there." The "there" characterizes the "disclosedness" and "openness" to the understanding of "being" in general. The fact *that* understanding and comprehending do take place makes it possible for the "openness" of the "there" to be "always already" opened up: this is the sense of "existence" as "exposure to beings."[5] Though Dasein and the human are not one and the same phenomenon, the notion of "openness" makes clear that only the human being can be Dasein. For Heidegger, animals are not in a position from which to understand "being."[6]

Thus, as he posits a particular "being," i.e., Dasein, as the bedrock of his investigation, Heidegger is trying to pose the question of the "meaning of being" and to get closer to an answer. For Dasein is the openness that makes the "understanding of being" possible. In this sense, it is the ground of the human rather than the human himself. This difference is essential because it opens a new chapter in the history of philosophy. Modern philosophy identified the ground of the human being with the human himself because it presupposed that the understanding of "being" was dependent on the faculties of human cognition. Since Descartes, the human being had been determined as the ground of "being," the "subject," that which lies at the basis of "beings" – *subiectum* means that which lies beneath or at the basis of something. By contrast, Dasein, as the ground of the question of the "meaning of being," is indeed a special or, as Heidegger says, an "exceptional being." Nevertheless, given that Dasein remains a "being" (*Seiendes*) with respect to "being" (*Sein*), as plants and animals also do, and given that we must say that both Dasein and animals "are," Dasein is not the ground of "being." Dasein is not the "subject," i.e., the instance of a universal measure from which all other "beings" can be derived. This distinction between Dasein and "subject" is also applicable to *Being and Time*, including the few passages where Heidegger uses the concept of the "subject" in an affirmative way.

Yet, even when considering Dasein as a "being," Heidegger still defines it as an "exceptional" being. This is an important nuance. Even as Heidegger's investigation in *Being and Time* abandons the point of view of Cartesian thinking, it does not entirely escape this tradition. This has to do with the fact that he characterizes "being" as *the transcendens pure and simple*.[7] As Heidegger will later write in the marginalia he added to this page, this *transcendens* – literally translated as what ascends beyond – is in fact not to be understood in a "scholastic and Greek-Platonic" manner as the absolute, i.e., as that toward which thinking is on the way when it leaves finite "beings" behind. Nevertheless, "every disclosure of being as the *transcendens*" is "transcendental knowledge," that is, a knowledge about the conditions of knowledge. (Later, looking back at *Being and Time*, Heidegger speaks at one point of an "exponential application of the transcendental question." Yet this "exponential application" is in no way an overcoming. Thus *Being and Time* did not abandon "the path of the transcendental formulation of the question.")

In order to be able to pose the question of the "meaning of being," Heidegger begins his investigation with Dasein. We must analyze characteristics of Dasein which shed light on the "meaning of being." Heidegger calls these characteristics "ways" or "modes of being." We can see Dasein's "ways of being" when Dasein becomes the "object" of philosophical reflection. The analysis is not supposed to alter the particular way in which Dasein happens. Thus Heidegger writes, "The manner of access and interpretation must instead be chosen in such a way that this being can show itself to itself on its own terms. And furthermore, this manner should show that being as it is *initially and for the most part* – in its average *everydayness*."[8] Dasein is supposed to "show itself in itself of its own accord." This is the untouched state, as it were, in which Dasein finds itself in the everyday. Thus Heidegger begins the "analytic of Dasein" by thematizing everyday praxis.

However, in the investigation of Dasein's everydayness, there is a presupposition at work that has far-reaching consequences. From the start, Heidegger seeks to consider Dasein as a "whole." At first glance, this "wholeness" appears to be a rather abstract characteristic of Dasein. The everyday seems scattered to us: I find myself involved in many unrelated activities. Accordingly, Heidegger speaks of the "phenomenal *manifoldness* of the constitution of the structural whole and its everyday kind of being."[9] Nevertheless, Dasein remains a unified "structural whole" in spite of all this scattering.

The "wholeness" of Dasein is, like its dispersion into the everyday, a temporal phenomenon. Dasein only becomes "whole" when it has come to its "end," i.e., when it has died. Because Dasein is a temporal unfolding, because it is finite and must die, it constitutes a unified "structure." Heidegger calls this "structural whole" "being-toward-death."[10] No matter how discontinuous Dasein's everyday existence may be, it is still able, because it has to die, to gather itself into a unity. Dasein is, as a "whole," "being-toward-death."

Heidegger orients his "analytic of Dasein" in terms of the central paradigm of everyday praxis. In the background of this orientation, we find the core thought of *Being and Time*. As Heidegger investigates the everydayness of Dasein, "temporality" shows itself as the "meaning" of Dasein.[11] However, "temporality" is Dasein's "meaning" only because we can, in and through this meaning, behold the question of the "meaning of being." "Temporality" is thus the "meaning" of Dasein because it is the first and ultimate "horizon of an understanding of being." Accordingly, the indirect goal of the analytic that immediately works out Dasein's everydayness is to contemplate time as the "horizon of being."[12] This is *Being and Time*'s true intention, namely, to elucidate the "meaning of being."

The orientation of the "analytic of Dasein follows the phenomenon which Heidegger had earlier called the "facticity of life." Therefore, given that everything "factically" lived is precisely something particular or individual, it makes sense for the analysis not to consider what the *general* subject of everydayness might be. Heidegger does not ask "what" everyday Dasein is but rather "*who* is it that Dasein is in its everydayness?"[13] This analytical displacement of the "what-question" to the "who-question" is anything but a marginal phenomenon. Without being able to delve extensively into the significance of this displacement, let us recall the following everyday situation:

> If we now encounter in our realm something like a human being as something strange, *how* do we ask toward him? We ask not indeterminately *what*, but *who* he is. We inquire about and experience the human being not in the realm of the What, but in the realm of the him and him, the her and her [*des Der und Der, der Die und Die*], of the *we*.[14]

Everyday Dasein is not the specimen of a genus nor the individual case of some general thing; rather, it is something particular and singular. Later, we shall have to ask whether

everyday Dasein must, in fact, always belong to a "we," i.e.,
a community.

The question of who everyday Dasein is already presupposes something that is obvious but important nevertheless.
We have already indicated that we must consider Dasein as
a "structural whole." Dasein does not attain this "wholeness"
only by "being-toward-death." At first, each individual Dasein
has to begin. As was the case with its end, Dasein is also
deprived of its beginning. Dasein enters the world as if it had
been "thrown into the deep end." Dasein is unable to begin
and at the same time desire and control this beginning; this
is what Heidegger calls "thrownness." Nevertheless, Dasein
is not simply thrown (*geworfen*). Besides the fact that Dasein
has to recognize that it is deprived of its own beginning
(thrownness), "projection" (*Entwurf*) is one of Dasein's possibilities. Though Dasein is unable to have control over its
beginning, it is nevertheless able to project what ensues from
this beginning, that is to say, it can give it a certain shape.
However, it is important to know that, for Heidegger, "projection" can never be completely detached from "thrownness."
Dasein cannot arbitrarily wish to be what or who it is. Thus
its existence comes to light as "thrown projection."

One aspect of "being-thrown" consists in the fact that
Dasein is originally and "always already" with others. Yet
we may not understand this originality as if Dasein were an
origin from which we could logically deduce "being-with-
others." At the origin, Dasein and "being-with-others" coexist
at the same time. To use a concept from Schelling's late thinking, Dasein and "other Daseins" are "equiprimordial." As
Heidegger puts it: "By taking our investigation in the direction
of the phenomenon which allows us to answer the question
of the who, we are led to structures of Dasein which are
equiprimordial with being-in-the-world: being-with and Dasein-
with."[15] Accordingly, Dasein is "always already" "being-with"
and "Dasein-with."

This sentence does not express a contingent or accidental
aspect of Dasein. "Being-with" and "Dasein-with" are ontological properties of Dasein. It belongs to the "understanding
of being" from the outset that Dasein lives with others. "Being-
with" is a characteristic of the "Dasein that is in each case
mine." "Dasein-with" characterizes other Daseins. Incidentally,

Heidegger does not think that other Daseins can be understood in terms of one's own Dasein. Here, we can only mention in passing that, for Heidegger, the other is not a "duplicate of the self."[16] However, to the extent that Dasein is originally "being-with," it can be there and "care" for others as "Dasein-with." "Care" is Dasein's distinctive "way of being."[17]

In everydayness, Dasein performs activities which make it possible for it to subsist. Dasein deals with things and "takes care" of them. This, too, is a structural aspect of Dasein. Dasein is essentially defined by this act of "taking care." "Care" is "the being of Dasein in general" precisely because "Dasein is concerned in its being *about* its being," because "care" points to the reflexive structure of the "self." Heidegger has called attention to the fact that "care" is not merely to be interpreted as a simple ordinary worry. Dasein "does not worry" but rather "takes care" of everyday matters and "cares" for others.

The most essential characteristic of "care" is that it rarely deals with past occasions and actions; nor does it primarily deal with present situations. The function of "care" is to orient Dasein toward the future. In "care," Dasein reaches, as it were, beyond itself toward that which announces itself and which may threaten Dasein. Even when nothing announces itself to Dasein nor threatens, Dasein still "cares" beyond itself. Dasein does not tend to its everyday affairs because each time some new eventual "worry" happens to arise. Rather, this is linked to a fundamental characteristic of Dasein. "Caring" Dasein fundamentally relates to what emerges from the "world" and comes toward it. "Caring," Dasein exists. Heidegger characteristically describes this openness to the future as follows: "The being of Dasein means being-ahead-of-oneself-already-in (the world) as being-together-with (inner-worldy beings encountered). This being fills in the significance of the term *care* [...]."[18] Dasein is always "ahead" of itself, it always relates to something whose presence is yet unfulfilled. Insofar as Dasein is "ahead" of itself, it is "next" to the things it has (and will have) to handle.

This "taking care" of everyday matters occupies Dasein in a specific way. At this point in the phenomenologico-hermeneutical survey of everydayness, Heidegger introduces a concept or, better put, a terminological distinction that still invites criticism today. First, let us recall that Heidegger indeed asked "who" Dasein is in the everyday. He now answers this question. Dasein's everyday "taking care" always happens in accordance with a particular "way of being." When I ride the bus or go to work, when I take out a loan or buy myself a pair of pants, I do all this as "they" do. In the everyday, that is, in the everyday public sphere, Dasein "takes care" of matters as "they" "take care" of matters. In the everyday, Dasein appears in the "way of being" of the "they."[19] Heidegger distinguishes this "way of being" from the possibility of "authentic" existence. Dasein "takes care" of everything it is "authentically" concerned with – like love or friendship, death or birth – in a different manner than when it "takes care of" everyday affairs. The "they" is the "neuter" of the everyday public sphere; by contrast, "authentic being-a-self" grants Dasein the possibility to live beyond everydayness.[20]

In *Being and Time*, Heidegger devotes much space to the description of the "they." The "they" is a "positive constitution of Dasein," that is to say, it necessarily belongs to it.[21] For Heidegger, the "mass society" of the twentieth century, together with its public sphere, is something new; the analysis of the "they" is Heidegger's attempt to describe the everyday of human beings in this new type of "mass society." With the "concept" of the "they," Heidegger approaches the phenomena of neutralization and functionality which Dasein must "factically" accept in the everyday. The "they" stands in for an anonymity without which we could not think the everyday of mass societies. At bottom, the "they" seems to provide a link to a political or sociological theory of the public sphere. From this point of view, Heidegger's analysis is not far from Rilke's description of the big city in *The Noteboooks of Malte Laurids Brigge* or Adorno's later remarks on the "culture industry."

However, as was already the case with Heidegger's interpretation of Paul, the reader may no longer remain naive vis-à-vis Heidegger's analysis of the "they." In a letter to his wife Elfride from 1916, Heidegger had already spoken of a "Jewification [*Verjudung*] of our culture and universities."[22] In those years, the link between Jewishness and the life in the big city was a common anti-Semitic stereotype. Not interested in farming the "native field," the Jew lives the mobile life of a tenant, manages the mass media, follows the flux of capital, and devotes himself to the modern inventions of art and science.

Is the "they," then, not a descriptive index of "Jewification"? The suspicion lies near at hand. Yet can it be confirmed?

The "they" is the Dasein that takes care of its everyday affairs. Thus the "they" makes it possible to describe the Dasein of everydayness. Dasein has the tendency to become absorbed in the everyday. Dispersion into the everyday is a possibility of life that Dasein desires: Dasein tends to lose and disperse itself into the "they." Heidegger writes: "The absorption of Dasein in the 'they' and in the 'world' taken care of reveals something like a *flight* of Dasein from itself as an authentic potentiality for being itself."[23] Dasein looks for possibilities to get out of the way; the evasion into the world of work and entertainment is one possible way of doing this. Heidegger calls this evasion "falling prey." Initially, as it "falls prey" to the world, Dasein has "always already" "fallen" out of itself. Dasein's tendency to disperse itself into the errands it takes care of is tantamount to a natural seduction (fallenness) on the part of the everyday.

Dasein flees from itself. There is a reason for this flight: as Dasein confronts itself, a particular "attunement" is brought about, namely, "anxiety."[24]

In fact, Heidegger thinks that anxiety is a "fundamental attunement" of Dasein. He distinguishes this "fundamental attunement" from "fear." "Fear" emerges when innerworldly beings, such as a mad dog, for example, threaten Dasein. By contrast, that "before which we have anxiety" is not an "innerworldly being."

In order to understand this difference between "fear" and "anxiety," let us rehearse a typical scenario of "anxiety": when I fear a dog, that which threatens me immediately stands before me. I can place it. In "anxiety," there is no such placement of myself and of what is threatening to me. A good horror movie nicely captures this experience. As in *The Blair Witch Project* (1999), what makes us anxious hardly appears. Yet authentic "anxiety" can even do without these traces. I have "anxiety" about my physical deterioration even before it has started. It is enough for me to think about it. Thus "anxiety" does not depend on the presence of any particular "being." This is, precisely, an important indicator of "anxiety" for Heidegger: "The fact that what is threatening is *nowhere* characterizes what anxiety is about."[25] We cannot locate "that before which we are anxious." This impossibility makes up the "positive" content of the phenomenon. This unlocatability is an aspect of anxiety: "Therefore, what is threatening cannot come closer from a definite direction within nearness, it is already 'there' – and yet nowhere. It is so near that it is oppressive and takes away one's breath – and yet it is nowhere."[26] What is "oppressive" (*was beengt*) gives us "anxiety." *Angst* and *Enge* are etymologically related.

"That before which" Dasein has anxiety is "nowhere"; this is an indication of its ontological status. "That before which" Dasein has anxiety is not a thing or an issue. Heidegger indicates this by means of an idiomatic expression: "When anxiety has subsided, in our everyday way of talking we are accustomed to say 'it was really nothing.'"[27] "That before which" Dasein has anxiety is really "nothing." What is this "nothing"? It is not an object or a "being." And yet it is something. This unobjectified something (the "nothing") is everywhere invisible. According to Heidegger, it is the "world": "In what anxiety is about, the 'it is nothing and nowhere' becomes manifest. The recalcitrance of the innerworldly nothing and nowhere means phenomenally that *what anxiety is about is the world as such*."[28] The "nothing and nowhere" is what is at stake in anxiety; it is "the world as such." The reason why the latter becomes manifest in such an oppressive way is because everything Dasein could possibly hold onto has dissolved into the "nothing."

Therefore, "anxiety" runs deeper than "fear." In "fear," Dasein deals with "beings." In anxiety, it is the "nothing" that is really at stake. Yet as Dasein deals with and is anxious about this "nothing," the "world as such" or – to quote the title of Peter Handke's book – "the weight of the world" becomes manifest.[29] Here, it is decisive that we do not interpret the "world" yet again as "a being" that would be different from Dasein: "So if what anxiety is about exposes nothing, that is, the world as such, this means that *that about which anxiety is anxious is being-in-the-world itself*."[30] Dasein is "being-in-the-world." "Anxiety" means that Dasein has to be there. In care, Dasein always relates to itself. It is clear, therefore, that Dasein is "anxious" about itself. The "they" abandons itself to the distraction of various forms of entertainment, it flees from itself because it is "anxious" about having to bear and endure "the weight of the world," i.e., itself.

In this respect, "anxiety" entails not only a "that before which" but also "an about which." These two terms are identical. When the "they" flees from "the weight of the world," it is anxious about losing the "world" or its "being-in-the-world": "Thus anxiety takes away from Dasein the possibility of understanding itself, falling prey, in terms of the 'world' and the public way of being interpreted. It throws Dasein back upon that for which it is anxious, its authentic potentiality-for-being-in-the-world."[31] At one and the same time, Dasein has "anxiety" before and about "authentic being-in-the-world." The structure of authentic threat is linked to this doubling. When Dasein has anxiety about life, what is threatening to it is both that which threatens it and its loss. Precisely via the analysis of "anxiety," *Being and Time* might establish a point of contact with Jacques Lacan's psychoanalytic theory, though Lacan's analysis of "anxiety" is more directly related to Kierkegaard.[32]

In "anxiety," it becomes clear to me the extent to which I am simultaneously anxious before and about my possibilities of life. Therefore, "anxiety" does not threaten my Dasein only on a case-by-case basis. In anxiety, Dasein's "wholeness" is at stake. The "fundamental attunement" of "anxiety" shows both that there is a "wholeness" of Dasein in general, and that this "wholeness" is a tenuous aspect. For the "nothing" before which Dasein is "anxious" proves to be the "possible impossibility of existence."[33] In an unequivocal way, "anxiety" makes Dasein accept the fact that it used to be whole at one point, and that means that Dasein will one day be gone. "Anxiety" shows that Dasein is "being-toward-death."

As Heidegger will say later, the human being is a "mortal."[34] With this definition, Heidegger picks up on an ancient thought. The Greek tragedians Aeschylus, Sophocles, and Euripides also referred to the human being as a mortal (*to thnēton, ho brotos*); here, humans and mortals are semantically identical. A saying from the Delphic oracle, an important source for Greek philosophy in general, confirms this definition of the human as mortal, in distinction to the immortal gods: "know thyself!" (*gnōthi seauton*), says the famous maxim which subsequently became part of the history of European thought. The oracle's saying attributes this maxim to Apollo. As the human being makes a pilgrimage to Delphi, he must, by contrast to the god, recognize himself as a mortal. Dasein is finite. All of Dasein's thoughts and actions have to correspond to this finitude. Should Dasein forget this finitude, the gods will remind it of it – as happens with the hubris of tragic heroes. Therefore, this knowledge of finitude is a self-knowledge. The analysis of *Being and Time* also gestures toward this connection.

There are different ways in which Dasein relates to "being-toward-death," which is "in each case mine." As the "mode of being" of the Dasein disperses into everydayness, the "they" evades "being-toward-death" and flees the "anxiety" that emerges when Dasein exposes itself to the "certainty" that it will die.[35] By contrast, "authentic Dasein" exposes itself to its own "being-toward-death." It "becomes free *for* its own death in anticipation," that is to say, it "anticipates death."[36] Because this "anticipation of death" liberates "inauthentic Dasein" from its everyday self-obfuscation, freeing it into "authentic Dasein," Heidegger is thus able to characterize it as "anticipatory resoluteness" (*vorlaufende Entschlossenheit*). "Authentic Dasein" finds itself "un-closed" (*ent-schlossen*), that is to say, it is necessarily delimited by its openness, mortality, and finitude. Dasein would not be an openness that relates itself to itself if "being-toward-death" did not delimit it.

"Being-toward-death" is "being-toward-the-end." Heidegger avoids the question of whether or not "something" could come after the end.[37] In this way, he opposes a philosophical tradition that has always affirmed the immortality of the soul over and against death. Whether it be Plato, who, in the *Phaedo* (in the dialogue of the dying Socrates), opens another perspective on the being of the soul beyond the body; or Aristotle, who takes philosophizing to be a participation in immortality, precisely; or Kant, who determines the immortality of the soul as a central problem of reason; or Hegel, who speaks dialectically of a "death of death"; philosophy has time and again not understood death as the absolute limit of the human. For Heidegger, however, Dasein's "authenticity" consists precisely in neither fabricating illusions beyond this limit nor thinking past it by means of strenuous theoretical efforts. By "anticipating death," "authentic Dasein" experiences its own limits, as well as the measure of time that originates in these limits.

As much as Heidegger's interpretation of Dasein as "being-toward-death" influenced generations of readers of *Being and Time*, it was just as often the object of criticism.

In the year of the publication of *Being and Time*, Max Scheler had already jotted down the following fragmentary note: "The first turn to the world is a matter of *Eros*, not anxiety, repulsion or flight."[38] In another place, he writes: "That which discloses a world to us is 'love' and not anxiety."[39] Scheler's criticism is directed at a tendency of the analytic of Dasein to overly individuate Dasein, severing it from any relation to the other. *Eros*, i.e., "love," is the "first turn" not just to the other but to world in general.

Decades later, a former student of Heidegger would pursue this critique further. Emmanuel Levinas emphasizes that the death which is "in each case mine" is not the "first death" that I encounter. He writes:

> Someone who expresses himself in his nudity – the face – is one to the point of appealing to me, of placing himself under my responsibility. Henceforth, I have to respond for him. All the gestures of other were signs addressed to me. […] The death of the other who dies affects me in my very identity as a responsible "me"; it affects me in my non-substantial identity, which is not the simple coherence of various acts of identification, but is made up of an unsayable responsibility. My being affected by the death of the other is precisely that, my relation to his death. It is, in my relation, my deference to someone who no longer responds, already a culpability – the culpability of the survivor.[40]

Levinas protests precisely the fact that Heidegger centers death and dying around the "Dasein that is in each case mine." Death is oppressive not because I will die, but rather because the other will. Insofar as we are "always already" responding to the other, there is an "unsayable responsibility" which is not interrupted in the face of death. It is in this sense that I'm still, as it were, responsible for the other's death. To the extent that I acknowledge this responsibility, I am there for the other.

This completely different type of phenomenology of death that Levinas proposes enables a new critical perspective on

Heidegger's analysis of "being-toward-death." Does the "analytic of Dasein" neglect the other and its death? Heidegger characterizes Dasein not only as a "being-toward-death" but also as "being-with." "Concern" (*Fürsorge*) is a mode of "care." Among other things, Heidegger defines it as the "concern that leaps ahead and frees."[41] This "authentic care" does not dissuade "Dasein-with" from his concerns but, instead, "helps the other to become transparent to himself *in* his care and *free for* it." The issue here is not to prevent the other from looking at his or her own death. "Authentic care" is supposed to make it impossible for others to evade death in the everyday and become blind to it. Contrary to Levinas, Heidegger's view is that the "first death" is "in each case mine": "*No one can take the other's dying away from him.* Every Dasein itself must take dying upon itself in every instance. Insofar as it 'is,' death is essentially each time my own."[42] For Heidegger, one's own death is the "first death." In fact, Heidegger would perhaps argue that it is knowledge of one's own death that first makes it possible to have a glimpse of death in general (and thereby of the death of the other as well). Nevertheless, Levinas is right to think that the notion of death is an index of the significance of the other pure and simple. My "care" for the other lives in the anxiety that the other might be wrenched away from me.

It was none other than Heidegger himself who limited the philosophical scope of *Being and Time*. He orients the main question of the book toward the "meaning of being," which is linked to the "horizon of time." In the last sentence of the book, we read: "Does time *itself* manifest itself as the horizon of being?"[43] This question gives us an indication that Heidegger limited the significance of the "analytic of Dasein." If time is the beginning of an answer to the question of the "meaning of being," would time not have to disclose immediate access to "being"? Would thinking not have to begin with time or "being itself" in order to grasp "time" and the "meaning" of "being"? Why must Dasein take up so much space in the question of the "meaning of being"? It would, of course, be problematic to ignore the relation between "being" and Dasein – a problematic undertaking that Heidegger attempts here and there in his thinking after *Being and Time*. The relation itself could not be severed. However, the last sentences of

Being and Time do announce a shift in emphasis vis-à-vis this relation. Later, Heidegger himself called this shift or inversion the "turn." After *Being and Time*, his thinking held fast to the relation between Dasein and "being." However, it no longer understood itself as the "analytic of Dasein" but instead as a "thinking of being."

Heidegger pursued this "thinking of being" to such an extent that he characterized the *"question of being"* – the question of the "meaning of being" – as the *"woodpath of my thinking."*[44] "Being as presence" (*Anwesen*) "led me astray" into thinking "being in terms of *'time.'*" However, the fact that the "question of being" is a "woodpath" is not an indictment against it. This notion stresses the aforementioned "path-like character" of Heidegger's thought. It is proper to this thought to put a question mark next to even its most fruitful insights.

The "ontological difference"

We have already mentioned the three most important fundamental concepts of Heidegger's thinking, namely, "being," "beings," and Dasein the "exceptional being." Even though they add up to three, these concepts clearly form a unity. At the same time, however, a difference becomes manifest. "Being" is not "a being." Heidegger initially characterizes this difference as the "ontological difference." It constitutes the fundamental structure of Heidegger's philosophy. Later, as with the question of the "meaning of being," Heidegger will subject the "ontological difference" to an important critique. An introduction to Heidegger's thinking reaches its limits in the explication of this fundamental structure. It is one of the hardest issues with which this thinking preoccupies itself. It takes time to understand it. One should not be discouraged if the first attempt is not successful. One becomes acquainted with philosophy – and not just Heidegger's philosophy – only by struggling repeatedly with it.

The lecture courses titled "The Basic Problems of Phenomenology" and "Introduction to Philosophy" – as well as the essay "On the Essence of Ground" – give us an account of Heidegger's first engagements with the "ontological difference," i.e., the distinction between "being" and "beings." In the first of these, a lecture course Heidegger gave in 1927, he writes:

> It is not without reason that the problem of the distinction between being in general and beings occurs here in first place. For the purpose of the discussion of this difference is to make it possible first of all to get to see thematically and put into investigation, in a clear and methodically secure way, the like of being in distinction from beings. The possibility of ontology, of philosophy as a science, stands and falls with the possibility of a sufficiently clear accomplishment of this differentiation between being and beings and accordingly with the possibility of negotiating the passage from the ontic consideration of beings to the ontological thematization of being.[45]

The formulation "the meaning of being" emphasizes the possibility of speaking about "being" (*Sein*), which is nothing like "a being" (*Seiendes*). As Heidegger questions this "meaning," he seeks to discuss "being itself." In *Being and Time*, however, Heidegger had argued that we can only answer this question if we begin by analyzing an "exemplary being." How does, then, the "passage" from the analysis of "a being" into the authentic "ontological thematization of being" happen? According to Heidegger, philosophy as "ontology" is not simply a "science" of "beings" but rather a "science" of "beings" in their relation to "being." The "passage" from the "ontic" to "ontology" has to do with this relation or comportment that Heidegger will thematize increasingly often.

In accordance with the methodological approach of *Being and Time*, an "ontological thematization" has to begin with the investigation of a particular "being," namely, Dasein. As Heidegger emphasizes in *Being and Time*, Dasein's "way of being" is grounded in "temporality." Thus Heidegger's first steps toward "ontological difference" led to an explanation of Dasein's specific "way of being," i.e., "temporality."[46]

In the course of the explication of "temporality" and its relation to Dasein, it becomes necessary for Heidegger to thematize "the basic condition for the knowledge of beings as well as for the understanding of being."[47] In this connection, he invokes Plato's allegory of the sun as presented in Book VI of the *Republic*. His suggestion is that "the passage from the ontic consideration of beings to the ontological the-matization of being" resonates with a basic principle of Platonic thought, namely, the notion that the good would go beyond even being itself and would thus be "beyond being." Thus Heidegger can say, "What we are in search of is the *epekeina tēs ousias.*"[48] The recurrence of this Platonic thought in the explication of "ontological difference" is very important. In his influential book *Plato's Theory of Ideas*, the new-Kantian Paul Natorp links the thought of a realm "beyond being" to the "concept of the transcendental" in the Kantian sense.[49] We can see traces of this in the Heideggerian notion of "onto-logical difference." It is perhaps no accident that, while living in Marburg, in the home of neo-Kantianism, Heidegger would then seek to carry out philosophy as ontology by means of a confrontation with Plato and Kant. Yet what resulted from this encounter was significantly different from the neo-Kantian thought of this period.[50]

The "fundamental condition" which makes it possible for Dasein to understand not only "beings" but "being itself" – which is not a being – is the existence of a realm that exceeds "beings" and discloses itself "beyond beings." Heidegger calls this realm "world." In "Introduction to Philosophy," the other lecture course mentioned above, he explains how the "ques-tion of being" is interwoven with the question of "world."[51] Just as Dasein "always already" has an "understanding of being," it also has a *"precursory understanding of world, i.e., significance."* This understanding, which allows Dasein to move in a leeway that transcends "beings," is in itself a *"genuine ontological meaning of transcendence."*[52] This means that Dasein *qua* "being-in-the-world" is able to soar beyond itself and "transcend" what is only present-at-hand or ready-to-hand.[53]

Yet another essential aspect of Platonic philosophy appears to be structurally analogous to the notion of "ontological difference." Especially as discussed in the *Phaedo* (67d), the concept of *chōrismos* – which points to the distinction or separation between body and soul – makes it possible to argue for the immortality of the non-corporeal soul in relation to the apparently deteriorating body. The concept of "ontological difference" echoes, as it were, this fundamental distinction in Plato's philosophy. Similar but not identical to the *epekeina tēs ousias*, the *chōrismo*s is a condition for "transcendence." It discloses a space that enables Dasein to transcend present-at-hand "beings" and leave them behind.[54]

Heidegger seeks to understand what is here conceived of as "transcendence" both starting from Kant *and* in opposition to the Kantian notion of the "transcendental." Kant indeed "came to recognize the problem of the 'transcendental' as a problem concerning the intrinsic possibility of ontology in general." However, the essentially "critical" significance Kant ascribes to the transcendental made it impossible for him to establish "a more originary elaboration of the idea of ontology, and thus of metaphysics, by means of a more radical and more universal conception of the essence of transcendence."[55] Here it is not possible nor conceptually necessary for us to delve more deeply into Heidegger's interpretation of Kant. Suffice it to register that, in the context of his first interpretation of the meaning of "ontological difference," Plato and Kant were the two thinkers Heidegger dealt with the most.

We have located the place where Heidegger first defines "ontological difference," that is to say, the point of departure for all other modifications of Heidegger's interpretation of the "ontological difference." In the essay "On the Essence of Ground," Heidegger points to the direction he thinks we should take: "we shall call this ground of the ontological difference the *transcendence* of Dasein."[56] The distinction between "being" and "beings" discloses the realm "beyond being," that is to say, the dimension of "world" or the "transcendence of Dasein."

During this period, Heidegger's explication of the "ontological difference" performs an epistemological function. Thus he is interested in grounding philosophy either as an "absolute science of being" or as "universal ontology."[57] This "absolute science" is *"transcendental science"* because its object is the world or "being" *qua* the openness of Dasein, i.e., "transcendence."[58] "Phenomenology" is supposed to be the method of this science.[59]

In the late 1920s, Heidegger pursued one of the philosophical strands of *Being and Time* by determining "phenomenology" as "universal ontology" or as "transcendental science." Heidegger's definition of philosophy as "universal ontology" runs counter to the concept of "worldview philosophy," which

Heidegger described as a "wooden iron," i.e., an oxymoron that combines mutually exclusive meanings. During this period, Heidegger engages with the concept of "worldview" as handed down by Kant and others.[60] Heidegger rejects the notion that philosophy is a "worldview," even though the latter "necessarily" belongs to Dasein. Like Husserl with his "transcendental phenomenology," Heidegger claims that "universal ontology" can lay a foundation for all the sciences.[61] Nevertheless, however clearly the program of scientific philosophy appears at this point in Heidegger's thinking, the problems that will lead this program into crisis are just as apparent. Let us now name and discuss at least two of these problems: the first one relates to the "universal" character of "being." Here, Heidegger does not thematize the concept of the "universal," whereas elsewhere he underscores an aspect of "being" which calls this "universality" into question. The other problem is to do with the "historicity" of Dasein, which we will consider in the next chapter.

Founding "universal ontology" is problematic because of the way in which "being" is, that is to say, because "being" is characterized by "withdrawal" or "concealment." Already in 1923, Heidegger writes, "Should it turn out that *to be* in the mode of covering-itself-up and self-veiling belongs to the character of the *being of being* – which constitutes the object of philosophy – and indeed not in an accessorial sense but in accord with the character of its being, then the category of 'phenomenon' will become a truly earnest matter."[62]

Heidegger argues that the category of "phenomenon" – that is, appearing in itself – only becomes a philosophical problem by means of a "self-concealment," i.e., a non-appearing. This seems to be a paradoxical thought which shows up again in *Being and Time*: Heidegger writes that a "phenomenon" is something that "does *not* show itself initially and for the most part, something that is *concealed* in contrast to what initially and for the most part does show itself."[63] The fundamental task of phenomenology is to behold this "concealment" or "self-veiling" that lies at the heart of all appearing. Thus the object of "universal ontology" is a non-object or non-phenomenon.

Over the course of the aforementioned "destructuring [...] of western philosophy," Heidegger remarks that, since Plato and Aristotle, metaphysical thinking has equated "being" with "presence."[64] Yet the consequences of this thought were not immediately recognizable. According to Heidegger, "self-concealment" makes up the "being-character of being." However, it is utterly impossible to understand "self-concealment" as "presence." The concealment of "being," by contrast, points to an elementary "absence", i.e., a "withdrawal." "Being itself" could no longer be conceived of as a self-stable entity. Had "western Philosophy" always somehow understood "being" as "a being"? Is it not the case that the "universal" character of this philosophy presupposes the stable "presence" of its basic principles? Heidegger realized that he had to bid farewell to this philosophical tradition. Thus he also had to abandon the thought that founding "universal ontology" was possible.

The notion of "ontological difference," i.e., the presupposition for Dasein's transcendence, suffers an important modification as a result of an insight that already appears in the last sections of *Being and Time*. Here, Heidegger refers to the "ontological enigma of the movedness of occurrence," that is, the "ontological enigma" of "history."[65] The enigma of this "movedness" prompted Heidegger to reconsider founding "ontology" on the basis of a Platonic and Aristotelian philosophical understanding. Heidegger began to doubt whether this philosophical understanding could match the authentic intentions of his thinking. This doubt led him to put forward a thought that strives to "overcome" the European understanding of philosophy as science of the first causes, i.e., "metaphysics." The "overcoming of metaphysics" is the thematic web from which we can explain the considerable transformations that the "ontological difference" undergoes. "Metaphysics" in general, and the distinction it makes between sensuous and supersensuous beings, seems to be grounded by the "ontological difference" without being aware of it.[66] It thus lies at the very heart of the matter that we cannot decide whether the "overcoming of metaphysics" – which still needs to be thought – correspondingly determines the "overcoming of the ontological difference," or if it is the other way around.

Contributions to Philosophy is a towering example of Heidegger's attempt to "overcome metaphysics," that is, the attempt to set the entire history of European thought on new and different paths. This text belongs to a set of works

designated as "treatises on the history of being." In *Contributions to Philosophy*, the "distinction" between "being" and
"beings" is the object of Heidegger's self-criticism:

> This distinction has been understood ever since *Being and
> Time* as the "ontological difference," and the aim has been to
> keep the question of the truth of beyng safe from all admixture.
> But this distinction is immediately applied to the path from
> which it originated. For there beingness comes to validity as
> *ousia*, as idea, and, in its train, as objectivity *qua* the *condition
> of the possibility* of an object.[67]

The "meaning of being" becomes the "truth of beyng." The
understanding of "ontological difference" as the basis for
Dasein's "transcendence" stops short of what Heidegger now
claims to think of as "the origin of ontological difference
itself, i.e., its genuine *unity*."[68] "Being itself" – which now
appears as "beyng" – remains distorted because it is stuck in
the "beingness of being" (*Seiendheit des Seins*), that is, in the
representational thinking of "that which is common to all
beings."[69] At the outset of his attempt to understand "ontological difference," as Heidegger let himself be guided by the
Platonic notion of *epekeina tēs ousias* on the one hand and
the Kantian theory of the "transcendental" on the other, that
which his thinking was on the way toward withdrew itself
from him: this was the "origin" of "ontological difference,"
which Heidegger now characterizes as the "essential occurrence" (*Wesung*) of beyng.[70]

As he now rejects Platonic and Kantian ideas, on account
of the fact that they (and their respective presuppositions)
cover over the "origin" or "genuine unity" of "ontological
difference," Heidegger positions himself earlier than, that is,
before, the age of Platonic-Aristotelian philosophy in order
to clarify his own philosophical views. He shows how the
forefathers of European philosophy fell prey to a peculiar
"forgetting." Even they were no longer able to understand
"being itself" as "being itself" and not as something like
"beingness," i.e., as the generality of "beings" such as the
idea or *ousia*, or as a particular being such as God. According
to Heidegger, this "forgetting" is not to be understood as a
type of amnesia. The issue is not that philosophers have "forgotten" "being" but that the "forgetting of being" – and the

adjacent notion of the "abandonment by being" – was made possible by a "truth of beyng" that withdraws and conceals itself.[71]

Heidegger displaces the notion of "ontological difference"; he sets the "ontological difference" in motion and reworks it in new ways time and again. The indication of an "origin" of "ontological difference" as its "unity" already makes clear that what is at stake here is not at all a binary structure. The "essential occurrence of beyng" as the "origin" of "difference" is that which is "between" "being" and "beings."[72] Here, we are dealing with a third structural factor. Therefore, what is at play in the distinction between "being" and "beings" is neither "being" nor "beings" but rather the "between" which unites and divides the two.

With the discovery of this "between," Heidegger tapped into a dimension scarcely accessible to the common ontological categories of interpretation. Thus the philosopher simply speaks of "difference *as* difference."[73] Difference is the "ground plan in the structure of the essence of metaphysics," though metaphysics cannot think it *as such*. As this "ground plan" is laid bare, the "overcoming of metaphysics" finds its guiding thread.

The striking concept of "ground plan" is meant to express two things. First, it points to the aforementioned notion that the entire history of "metaphysics," together with the metaphysical distinction between sensuous and supersensuous beings – or, if you will, the distinction between "idealism" and "materialism" – is based on this "ground plan" (*Grundriss*). Thus it becomes clear that the "ground" of European thought is a "rift" (*Riss*). It is impossible to deepen or cancel out this "rift" into a "unity" or "identity." Nevertheless, European thought tends to affirm the stable "presence" of its essential categories. Should this thought be grounded on nothing other than "difference as difference," it would then have to be the case that the notion of stable entities – and their operative conceptuality – is in fact unfounded.

Yet the "path-like character" of Heidegger's thinking encompasses precisely its most central aspects. As the "question of being" turns into a "woodpath," the "ontological difference" also shows itself in a new light. Heidegger describes it as a "barrier that blocks a path."[74] Thus in the late 1950s

Heidegger arrives at the notion of "abandoning" or "destructuring the ontological difference." He no longer relates this "destructuring" to "western philosophy" and its "inception." What is at stake here is no longer a "retrospective look at the inception" but an "anticipatory glance at the inception, i.e., the event of appropriation as that which remains to be thought." Stressing the verb "let," Heidegger speaks here of "letting essences essence," that is to say, the "event of appropriation." The latter is no longer to do with the "question of being." In the sentence, "The being of beings means the essencing of essences," essencing is attributed to essences as their predicate. "Essencing" would then be something "accidental to essences." Thus thinking would remain "stuck on a sentence about being that treats being as something accidental." In order to come closer to the "issue at hand," i.e., the "event of appropriation," Heidegger had to abandon the "question of being" and, with it, the "ontological difference."

In a new and thoroughly esoteric style, Heidegger now tries to grasp "difference as difference" (*Differenz als Differenz*). The key German word Heidegger uses for difference is *Unterschied*. It is the "divide [*Schied*] of the between" that announces a "relation to the between which has not yet been clarified." This "between" is the so-called "time-space that determines the field of projection of essencing and objectivity."[75] The "abandonment by being" is now the "same" as the "forgetting of dif-ference [*Unter-schied*]."

Many philosophers have taken up Heidegger's thinking of the "ontological difference." Already in *Of Grammatology*, Jacques Derrida draws attention to the fact that, for Heidegger, the "meaning of being is not a transcendental or trans-epochal signified."[76] Rather, Derrida calls the "meaning of being" a "determined signifying trace." This means that "within the decisive concept of ontico-ontological difference, *all is not to be thought at one go*." The notion of the "ontico-ontological" is derivative with regard to difference. Derrida himself speaks of *différance*, which he calls an "economic concept" since it designates the "production of *différer*" in the two senses of this French verb, namely, "to defer" and "to differ." Whoever seeks to engage with Derrida's project of "deconstruction" has to rely on an understanding of "*différance*." In the same year of 1967 – which was such a decisive year for Derrida

– he shows in "Violence and Metaphysics" that, contra Levinas, it is not possible to think through ethics, and a fortiori Levinasian ethics, without the "ontological difference," i.e., the "thinking of being."[77] In a critical way, Derrida emphasizes that the "ontological difference" is "the more original difference" in comparison to the "difference" with the Other.[78] The notion of "difference as difference" is applied in an ethical context.

The ethical significance of the thought of "difference as difference" consists in the fact that, over and against the tradition of European philosophy, "difference" is no longer subordinated to its counter-concept of "identity." Classical European philosophers have often construed the phenomenon of the other and of otherness as something which would have to be sublated (and thus overcome) by a first and last identity, i.e., a "totality" which unites everything. Something very different is at stake when "difference as difference" is the "ground plan of thinking." However, not enough critical attention has been paid to Heidegger's own statements about ethics.[79] There are tendencies in Heidegger's thinking that run counter to the elaboration of an ethics.

The "historicity" of Dasein

At its early stage, Heidegger's philosophizing was keen to reflect on the importance that primordial Christian religiosity and Greek philosophy had for the "facticity of life." The "concept of the historical" is "*a core phenomenon*" and already plays a major role here.[80] As Heidegger delves into an exploration of the "meaning" of "history" within the context of the "analytic of Dasein," this phenomenon becomes unquestionably important for him. What Heidegger had to accomplish in *Being and Time* was to exhibit the systematic nexus between Dasein and "history" within the purview of the question of the "meaning of being."

Heidegger specifies the extent to which the "way of being" of "care" points to the "wholeness" of Dasein. In "care," Dasein relates to itself. It takes care of its affairs in order to secure its future. Thus it is "always already" beyond itself, relating itself to what is yet to be. Even "concern," which deals with others, reaches into the future. This movement of Dasein – according to which it unfolds from what it has been into what it will be – is the "happening" (*Geschehen*) which Heidegger understands ontologically as "history" (*Geschichte*), i.e., the "historicity" of Dasein. "Temporality" is therefore the "condition of possibility" for Dasein to exist "historically."[81]

The "historicity" of Dasein can be viewed from two different perspectives. In a manner that we still have to explain, Dasein is able to comport itself "authentically" to "history." On the other hand, Dasein can take up an "inauthentic" relation to "history" and remain completely unware of "historicity." Heidegger's later statements about the "lack of history" go further still.

As Dasein comes to recognize a "heritage" in "history," it arrives at a "resolute" relation to "history," that is to say, it reaches its "actual factical possibilities of authentic existing."[82] "Everything 'good' is a matter of heritage, the character of 'goodness' lies in making authentic existence possible." Dasein must recognize and appropriate the "possibility of authentic existing." This takes place as a "retrieval."[83] Here, "to retrieve" (*Wiederholung*) does not mean "to repeat" but rather to fetch back (*zurückholen*) the possibilities of action that Dasein thinks it is possible to retrieve – the whole of *Being and Time* begins with an "explicit retrieval of the question of 'being.'"[84] Naturally, this "retrieval" cannot possibly include everything that happened in the past. In "renunciation," Dasein is able to relate to history in a critical manner.[85] As it "renounces" certain past events, Dasein shows itself to be responsible for its "heritage." However, the meditation of its "heritage" is only the beginning of Dasein's "authentic historicity."

The "anticipation of death" entails the "resoluteness" with respect to "tradition."[86] "Only being free *for* death gives Dasein its absolute goal and pushes existence into its finitude." In this way, Dasein attains "the simplicity of its *fate*." The Dasein that conceals "finitude" from itself relates to history in an indifferent way. As Dasein abandons itself to the "inauthentic" praxis of the "they," it does not accede to "tradition." Only when Dasein grasps its "finitude" does it leave its everyday indifference behind. Dasein "chooses" the "possibilities" that "tradition" has handed down to it. Dasein then achieves a "goal," that is to say, it finds "its fate."

For Heidegger, "death" is the "power" by means of which "Dasein understands itself in its own *higher power* of its finite freedom."[87] Dasein's "higher power" consists in "taking over the *powerlessness* of being abandoned to itself" and "becoming lucid about the chance elements in the situation disclosed." As Dasein "anticipates death" and carries out "finitude," it becomes, as it were, sensitive to events that either stem from or correspond to its heritage. "Historicity" becomes a determining factor of concrete action. Moreover, Dasein is never alone in its comportment toward its "heritage." This is to do with the fact that "fateful Dasein essentially exists as being-in-the-world as being-with-others." Therefore, Dasein's "happening" (*Geschehen*) is a "happening-with" that Heidegger understands as "destiny" (*Geschick*). The latter is the "happening of a community or of a people." Thus Dasein's "historicity" entails that Dasein "always already" belongs to a "community," i.e., a "people" (*Volk*).

This fundamental and ontological – and, as we shall see, problematic – discussion of "historicity" resonates widely through the whole of Heidegger's philosophy. An immediate consequence of this knowledge is the far-reaching distinction between "history" (*Geschichte*) and "historiography" (*Historie*).[88] Historiography appears as an objectification of a fundamental "way of being" of Dasein. The "science of history" objectifies that wherein Dasein "always already" exists. Thus Heidegger acknowledges that this science is, in a certain way, necessary for Dasein's understanding of itself. Over the course of his thinking, however, Heidegger increasingly contested the claim that historiography is able to research history. Accordingly, ten years after *Being and Time*, in the "treatise on the history of being" titled *Mindfulness*, Heidegger writes:

> The consequence of the political-historiographical conception of modern man is that only with the help of this conception will historicism be brought to completion. Historicism is the total domination of historiography in the sense of reckoning with what is past in view of what is present with the claim to specify thereby once and for all the essence of man as something historiographical and not historical.[89]

Whereas linking historiography back to the "analytic of Dasein" was one of the main objectives of *Being and Time*, Heidegger will later deny historiography the possibility of grasping history. A methodological tendency that is perhaps particular to the "science of history," namely the leveling down of epochal differences – are Neanderthals and the Ancient Greeks equally important in the context of the European interpretation of the self? – provoked a highly idiosyncratic Heideggerian critique. The explication of Dasein's "historicity" in *Being and Time* obviously has to be at odds with the methodological indifference of a "science of history." The historian definitely does not need to "anticipate death" in order to plan his research.

A further consequence of Heidegger's thorough engagement with history is that, after *Being and Time*, he no longer understands "historicity" simply as a "way of being" of Dasein but rather relates it to "being itself." Already in *Being and Time* he writes that "questioning being [...] is itself characterized by historicity."[90] The way in which we philosophically thematize "being itself" is "historically" decided. At first glance, it looks as though Heidegger were making "being" into a higher entity which would dispatch itself differently across various epochs and would thus have to be regarded as the "ground" of history. In *Contributions to Philosophy*, he writes: "History can be grounded only in the essence of beyng itself, i.e., only in the relation of beyng to the human being who is equal to that relation."[91] Nevertheless, this relation of grounding is not applicable to "being" and history because it is not possible to localize it beyond "temporality" or beyond history. Such a schema would get us back to the Hegelian differentiation of an eternal "Spirit" that "falls into time." For Heidegger, on the contrary, "being" and "history" are inextricably linked in the sense that "being" at once is and is not "history." This ambiguity is apparent in the "beyng-historical genitive" of Heidegger's phrase "history of being": "history" is "the event of appropriation" of "being itself."[92] "Being itself" decides what "history" is.

Examined more closely, we can see that the relation of grounding between "temporality" and "historicity" – as presented in *Being and Time* – has now become untenable. If our conception of "temporality" is *itself* able to change "historically," it is then no longer possible to interpret "temporality," i.e., "being," as the "condition for the possibility" of history. In his early interpretation of Paul, Heidegger indicates that "primordial Christianity" "lives" "time itself." As primordial Christianity grasps "temporality" in an "eschatological" way – as it awaits the Parousia – this then totalizes a "historical" conception of "temporality" as "time itself." In the context of this totalization of "historicity," it would seem as though Heidegger's later thinking privileged the possibility of relating our conception of "temporality" back to a "historical" narrative (or a myth). This notion hints at what Heidegger calls the "other inception" from 1932 onward.

With the final chapters of *Being and Time*, Heidegger's thinking heralds a *totalization of history* that will have devastating consequences. This totalization also appears in texts that had hitherto generally been regarded as unproblematic. It is inscribed, for example, in the masterful 1929 essay "On the Essence of Ground," written in commemoration of Edmund Husserl's seventieth birthday. There, Heidegger specifies that "*in* this surpassing," i.e., "transcendence," "Dasein for the first time comes toward that being that *it* is, and comes toward it *as* it 'itself.'"[93] Heidegger uses the concept of the "self" in an ambiguous way before making it clearer in the lectures and essays from 1933.[94] On the one hand, Dasein's "self" simply points to the fact that Dasein, as opposed to all other "beings," is able to relate to itself. On the other hand, the "self" can be understood as a "figure" of "authenticity," so that "fate" and "destiny" become inscribed in Dasein's reflexive relation to itself. The "self" is now a placeholder for "identity." Heidegger never got around to articulating this distinction in a more precise way.

The philosophical problem with the concepts of "historicity," Dasein, "fate," and "destiny" – terms that today we rightly regard with a great deal of caution – lies in the fact that, in acting "historically," Dasein becomes the representative of a "people" (*Volk*) which, like Dasein itself and its "self," cannot be pluralized. Like the individual Dasein, a "people" speaks in *one* voice. It is only in this way that it can have a "destiny," which is always *one* "destiny." Because such a "destiny" is what is always apparently at stake in "history," whatever is against this "destiny" can only ever stand outside of history. After World War II, this is precisely the accusation Heidegger makes against those "who stood beside us, in the realm of spinelessness."[95] In other words, for Heidegger, there could not possibly have been an alternative to the revolution – i.e., the "destiny" – of 1933.

Heidegger dates the exact period of his support of National Socialism back to the years of 1930–4.[96] During this period, he "saw in National Socialism the possibility of a transition to another inception and interpreted it in that way." Later on, Heidegger himself told Karl Löwith, one of his Jewish students, that *Being and Time*'s explication of "historicity" played a role in this. Löwith reports that he once put to Heidegger his view that the latter's involvement with National Socialism lay "in the essence of his philosophy."[97] According to Löwith, Heidegger agreed with him "without hesitation," adding that "his concept of 'historicity' formed the basis of his political engagement." From this perspective, we can understand Heidegger's "engagement" with National Socialism as a logical and conscious development of his thought.

"Philosophical life in Germany" took its course. On April 21, 1933, Heidegger was appointed rector of Freiburg University. On April 23, 1934, he offered his resignation. Still, this tells us nothing yet.

3

The "History of Being"

How can one know what history is if one does not know
what poetry is [...]?[1]

Hitler and the "other inception"

The great experience and fortune that the Führer has
awakened a new actuality, giving our thinking the correct
course and impetus.[2]

Around 1930, Heidegger begins to draw certain consequences
from ideas developed especially in *Being and Time*. The "question of being" is "itself characterized by historicity."[3] The issue
now is to grasp "historicity" not simply as a "way of being"
of Dasein but rather as a "way of being" of "being itself,"
as it were. This reorientation of Heideggerian thought, often
shorthanded as the concept of the "turn," does not simply
reverse the relation between "being" and "beings." We must
instead realize that, at the "turn," the thought of a "history
of being" transposes Dasein's "historicity" onto "being."

To think the "history of being" means to grant "being" a
"history." This is how Heidegger began in the early 1930s.
Later on, he would characterize this first step in the following
manner: "from the hermeneutic of '*Da-sein*' to the mytho-logy

of the event of appropriation."[4] This incomplete sentence seems to relate to two stages in Heidegger's thought. In *Being and Time*, thinking questioned the "meaning of being" by taking Dasein as its point of departure. In the "history of being," thinking questions the "truth of beyng" from out of the horizon of the "event of appropriation." The latter is now determined as a "mytho-logy."

In a lecture course from the winter semester of 1933–4, Heidegger characteristically meditates on the difference between *logos* and *muthos*. *Logos* is to be understood as a gathering which "pertains to the With and the Together of beings."[5] *Muthos* is "the word that comes upon human beings and indicates this and that about the entirety of human Dasein; it is not the word in which human beings give their account of things, but rather the word that gives them a directive."[6] Language first becomes *logos* "through and with philosophy." However, the "originary *logos* of philosophy remains bound to *muthos*; only with the language of science is the bond dissolved." It is in this sense that *logos* and *muthos* are mutually intertwined in philosophy: "mytho-logy."

The problem associated with this commitment to *muthos*, i.e., to storytelling or narrative, becomes clear if we consider Aristotle's *Poetics*. Tragedy is the imitation of an action that transmits itself as *muthos*, the soul of tragedy (*psuchē tēs tragōdias*). Every action would be a whole. A whole, however, has a beginning, middle, and end (1450 b26). To the extent that Heidegger grants "being" a history or *muthos*, he has to ascribe to this history certain formal elements which, as a narrative, cannot but be founded on the authoritative function of the author himself. In other words, Heidegger's "history of being" cannot be anything less than a narrative of the author Heidegger who constantly unauthorizes himself.[7]

The lecture course of the summer semester of 1932 makes this immediately apparent. There, at the very beginning, Heidegger speaks of the "end of metaphysics" and of the "other inception of western philosophy" in the pre-Socratic thinkers, Anaximander and Parmenides.[8] During the lecture course, it becomes clear that what is at play here is not the more or less conventional distinction between an "inception" with the Greeks and an "end" in the European present. This idea is undermined by Heidegger's injunction to "begin with the inception."⁹ The "inception" is doubled. Thus Heidegger speaks of a "first inception" and of *the re-inception of the initial inception*."¹⁰ This "other inception" or "re-inception" is characterized as what is "primarily decisive" for us "today."¹¹ However, this "re-inception" necessarily leads us back to the "end." Heidegger speaks of the "mission" to bring about the "cessation of philosophy."¹²

In the summer of 1932, this interpretation of "inception" and "end" corresponds to political hopes that Heidegger harbored at the time. *Ponderings II* and *III*, two volumes of the *Black Notebooks* written in the early 1930s, bear witness to this in their own way. Whereas Heidegger initially remains silent as to his political hopes, the entries become more explicit from the "fall of 1932" onward – though Heidegger had already stated his revolutionary position before this time: "When will we finally play and play on to the struggle? / Enough of tuning and burnishing! Or indeed not enough? / And in all this only a *writer* of words."¹³ In an entry that recalls the "inception," he writes: "The great experience and fortune that the Führer has awakened a new actuality, giving our thinking the correct course and impetus."¹⁴

Heidegger deemed National Socialism to be "the possibility of a transition to another inception." The "transition" (*Übergang*) is not yet the "other inception" (*Anfang*) itself. This distinction captures quite well Heidegger's position. The Nazi "seizure of power" (*Machtergreifung*) is not yet the "empowerment of being."¹⁵ The "national revolution" is not yet *the* "revolution" which the philosopher would later, in a "revolutionary way," describe as "the essential revolt back to the inceptive."¹⁶ Over and against historical "revolutions," he opposes revolutions "in the history of being": "no 'revolution' is 'revolutionary' enough."¹⁷

Be that as it may, Heidegger is prepared to support historical events with his thinking. His appointment as rector of Freiburg University, which he accepted "against" his "innermost voice," plays a lesser role in this.¹⁸ What is more astonishing is the verve with which Heidegger carries over the revolutionary situation into his thinking. We must bring "philosophy" to an "end" and thereby "prepare what is wholly other," i.e., "metapolitics." Accordingly, a *"transformation of science"* would also be necessary; incidentally, Heidegger

himself never really managed to clarify – not even in a preliminary fashion – this idea or the extreme demands it entailed.

There is hardly any information on this "metapolitics."
Nevertheless, Heidegger suggests that the "metaphysics of
Dasein" that he had worked out in the end of the 1920s had
to "become deeper in accord with the innermost structure of
that metaphysics and expand into the metapolitics 'of' the
historical people." The object of this "metapolitics" is the
"historical people," i.e., the Germans – and the Germans only
– who in turn elaborate this "metapolitics." The fact that
Heidegger does not further define the concept of "metapolitics"
does not mean that this concept was not developed in his
writing. On the contrary, it is possible to argue that precisely
the notebook entries of the first *Ponderings* – and not only
this text – fall under this "metapolitics."

The main exoteric text that publicly describes this "metapolitics" is the Rectorial Address, the lecture titled "The Self-
Assertion of the German University," held at the Maximum
Auditorium of Freiburg University on May 27, 1933. The
Address picks up on a theme that had already interested Heidegger in texts from before 1930. The "historicity of Dasein"
– a phase of the "metaphysics of Dasein" – concerned itself
first and foremost with Dasein's relation to its "self," a relation
not in the abstract or reflexive sense but rather as a relation to
a "self" that implicates the whole of life's "facticity." When it
is a matter of founding an "inception," Heidegger evokes the
question of the "self": "But do we know *who we ourselves
are* [...]? *Can* we know that at all, without the most constant
and most uncompromising and harshest *self-examination*?"[19]
It is not solely for rhetorical purposes that the discourse is
written in the first-person plural. Rather, in saying that Dasein's "self" can only be clarified in terms of Dasein's belonging
to a "people," Heidegger remains faithful to the concept of
"destiny" that he had introduced in *Being and Time*.

Heidegger summarizes what this belonging ought to show
us in the most important conclusions of the Address: "The
three bonds – *through* the Volk *to* the destiny of the State *in*
its spiritual mission – are *equiprimordial* with the German
essence. The three forms of service that follow from them

– labor service, military service, and knowledge service – are equally necessary and of equal rank."[20]

"Bonds" and "services" are related to one another. The belonging to a "people" is attested daily by "labor service," while the participation in the State of this people is attested by "military service." Ahead of these two "bonds," the "spiritual mission" consists in "knowledge service."[21] The unified origin of the unfolding of "bonds and services" is the "German essence." This formulation already provides a direction in which the answer to the question of "who we ourselves are" will lie. We must note, however, that Heidegger was always more interested in the question of "essence" – or, better put, in the *performative act of questioning* the essence – than in its answer. This leads to the paradoxical statement that the "essence of the Germans" lies in the "*struggle* [*Kampf*] over their essence."[22]

Heidegger pursues two concrete projects: "Supposing the spiritual power is sufficient, then only *two things* could help a forward movement: (1) the new construction of one sole university (2) in unity with that, a teachers' school."[23] The centralization of the "knowledge service" in *one* university was meant to accomplish the goal of training teachers for the whole *Reich*. Heidegger even worked out a few directives for this.

The philosopher realized fairly quickly, however, that the "Spiritual National Socialism" that he opposed to the actual "Vulgar National Socialism" was an absurd project.[24] It did not take long for him to characterize his rectorship as a "great mistake."[25] The retreat from actual politics followed immediately after.

Of course, this does not mean that Heidegger gave up his interest in National Socialism. On the contrary: the motives for his retreat are ambivalent. At first, Heidegger adopts the typical position of a revolutionary for whom the revolution is never carried out in a sufficiently radical way. It is in this sense that, in a non-pejorative way, he characterizes "National Socialism" as a "barbaric principle,"[26] that is, "its essential character and its possible greatness." It is not National Socialism that is the "danger" but its watering down. And, indeed, his ideas for a "transformation of science" did not find a fertile soil. The members of the Party had no understanding of Heidegger's rather unclear yet very radical agenda.

Later on, emphatically reevaluating this situation, Heidegger declares that a "mere 'revolution' in beings without a transformation of beyng creates no originary history but simply entrenches what is already present-at-hand."[27] Thus there would not be an "*im*mediate" link between Heidegger's thinking and National Socialism. In a "mediate" way, however, both converge on "a decision concerning the essence and destiny of the Germans and thus press toward the fate of the West." If Heidegger maintained a certain loyalty to National Socialism, and thus to the "Third Reich" of the National Socialists, until the end of the war, this had to do with this "being-historical" (*seinsgeschichtlich*) narrative. It was up to the Germans to fulfill the "destiny of the West" by means of a "transformation of beyng."

It is not easy to parse the distance-taking strategy of Heidegger's interpretation of what was then called the "National Revolution." His reasons for changing his views stem from the recognition that a coincidence between the "'revolution' in beings" and the "transformation of beyng" was an "error" – and not simply because the "'revolution'" left "beings" intact. Heidegger realized that National Socialism was among the phenomena that were an obstacle to the "transformation of beyng." "National Socialism," just like "Bolshevism," embodies "machinational victories of machination – gigantic forms of the consummation of modernity."[28] Heidegger's "being-historical" interpretation dislodges National Socialism from its narrative function of heralding the "inception," making it instead a representative of the "end."

One consequence of this is that the "transformation of beyng," i.e., the "other inception," also had to be deferred. Heidegger recognized that the "modern age" – which he thought National Socialism had put an end to – still needed to go through National Socialism itself. This, then, is the basis for the thought that a merely moralistic critique of National Socialism would be pointless within a "being-historical" context. What's more, the collapse of National Socialism before its "consummation" would foreclose the possibility of a "transformation of beyng." Heidegger deduces from this the "necessity of affirming National Socialism."[29] When

Heidegger takes the historical events of war and mass murder into account without moralistically condemning them, when he in fact affirms them in a "being-historical" way, he means it in the sense that, within the "mytho-logy of the event of appropriation," the "consummation of modernity" had to be fully carried out, *without remainder*. A full night first had to fall so that a new morning could then dawn. The image of light shining only in darkness belongs to the "heritage" of Christianity (cf. John I: 5).

Heidegger will likewise characterize the "role of nationalisms" as the "incitement of imperialism."[30] "Socialism" is the "expansion of imperialism." The "empowerment of imperialism" is synonymous with the "conducting of humanity to unconditional machination," i.e., technology.[31] The latter employs "an irresistible lure": it "grants the executors of machination the consciousness" to freely carry out their intentions. "In truth, the surrender of imperialism into unconditional slavery to machination has already been decided." This took place in the "anteroom of the history of beyng," within which "we draw near to the *western revolution*." This "revolution" is not yet the "other inception" but rather the "*ending*" as the "verge of a prospective decision between nothingness and beyng."[32] But this "ending" had to take place in order for the "other inception" to be possible.

Heidegger interpreted World War II to be a sign of this "ending." The greater and the more destructive the war becomes, the closer Heidegger thinks we are to the changeover of the "transformation of beyng." Every actor in the war "becomes a slave of the history of beyng, a history for which right from the beginning they were judged to be too small and so were compelled into war."[33] In war, only "beings" fall victim to annihilation. For war is "never the begetter and master of *beyng* – but always only of *beings*."[34] "Beyng" is "incomparable and nonrelational." The events in the course of which millions of people were annihilated could not have affected "beyng" in the slightest.

Between 1930 and 1934, Hitler was for Heidegger the guardian of the National Socialist revolution which could have enabled the transition into the "other inception." After 1934, Heidegger began to make a distinction between the possibilities of this "revolution" and its actual reality. He then realized that the reality of National Socialism was nothing but a necessary epochal phase in the "history of being" that still had to be carried out. Heidegger took the catastrophic dimension of World War II to be the consummation of this phase. Hitler appeared to be not the "inception" but the "end." Yet the "history of being" decided otherwise.

"Hölderlin and the Germans"

> I have the feeling that another hundred years of neglect are needed before people start realizing what Hölderlin's poetry holds in store.[35]

The title of this section refers to a lecture that Norbert von Hellingrath, the first editor of a historico-critical edition of the collected writings of Friedrich Hölderlin, gave in Munich in 1915.[36] Though Heidegger never makes reference to this lecture, in it Hellingrath – "who, at the age of 28, was killed in action at Verdun in 1916" – interpreted Hölderlin in a manner that anticipated and influenced the philosopher in a marked way.[37] In many places, Heidegger is critical of Hellingrath's editorial decisions. However, in a passage written after World War II, we read that Hellingrath was someone who "loved the letter, that is to say, who could be a philologist solely because he loved destiny."[38] Here, "destiny" does not mean the "happening of community, of a people" – as it did in *Being and Time* – but rather the "destiny of beyng."[39] In the narrative of this "destiny," the Germans were supposed to play a major role. Who were these "Germans"?

After stepping down as rector in 1934, Heidegger gives a lecture titled "Logic as the Question of the Essence of Language." The title contains a critique. In the 1933–4 lecture course of the previous winter semester titled "On the Essence of Truth," Heidegger had already established that "reflection on *logos* as the theory of *language*, that is *grammar*, is dominated at the same time by logic as the theory of thinking."[40] By "*destabilizing the grammatical representations of language*," we must bring an end to the dominion of "logic."[41] This can only happen if the "essence of language" is thematized.

At the end of the summer semester lecture course of 1934, this "destabilization" is achieved. Heidegger writes: "The essence of language essences where it happens as world-forming power, that is, where it in advance performs and brings into jointure the being of beings. The original language is the language of poetry."[42] A definite orientation is thus given, and not only to the problematization of the "essence of language." Heidegger speaks at the same time of a "poet" whose name he keeps secret. "Poetry and, with it, proper language happens only where the ruling of being is brought into the superior untouchability of the original word." If the Germans wished to "grasp" this, they would have to "learn what it means to preserve that which they already possess." For Heidegger, the place where the "ruling of being" is brought to language is Hölderlin's poetry, a "possession" of the "Germans."

To a careful auditor of Heidegger's lecture courses, it should come as no surprise that Heidegger would go on to read Hölderlin's poetry in the winter of 1934–5, more especially Hölderlin's hymns "Germania" and "The Rhine." With this first interpretation of Hölderlin, Heidegger's philosophy undergoes a change in orientation, the importance of which one could hardly overestimate. Seen from the perspective of *Being and Time* and the ensuing lecture courses, one could in fact say that Heidegger's first lecture course on Hölderlin – as the beginning of his lifelong interpretation of Hölderlin that followed him even to his grave – disclosed to his thinking a new and thoroughly problematic dimension.[43]

Heidegger's interest in Hölderlin can be explained from several perspectives. Philosophically speaking, Heidegger did not give the problem of "language" its due in *Being and Time*.[44] In the context of the question of the "historical" status of philosophy, "logic" – what it is and is not – had to be discussed. It was in this way that the importance of a focused meditation on "language" became clear for Heidegger. Language was then linked to the problem of "historicity" and actualized by the interest in "metapolitics."

Hölderlin is immensely important for Heidegger on many levels. First, he plays a pivotal role in Heidegger's question of the "essence of language." This role then makes him the epicenter of "the metapolitics 'of' the historical people." Over and beyond this, Hölderlin provided the most important

orientations in Heidegger's narrative of the "history of being."
As a poet, he participates in the project of "overcoming metaphysics" and discloses a singular perspective to Heidegger's
thinking of technology.

We readily understand poetry as a creative activity which
"creates its works in the realm of language and out of the
'material' of language."[45] We receive poems as works of art
that communicate the subjective experiences of the poet. At
the same time, European culture shows us that poetry can
go beyond this definition. Since the Homeric epics, poetry
is conceived not only as a linguistic art form – made from
linguistic material – but also as a signifying nexus on which
identities are founded. The latter provided the "Greeks" with
an orientation in the world. Homer's stories about the gods
were particularly binding for them. Plato, too, has to con-
front Homer first in order to legitimate philosophy as an
authentic way to interpret the cosmos. The Christian world
also has to rely on poetry in its self-understanding, given
that some of the most canonical Christian texts are great
poems.

In this way, poetry is something more, or other, than the
creative activity of an individual that expresses himself. It
offers a community the possibility of self-understanding. In
the aforementioned 1934 summer lecture course, Heidegger
attributed this significant role to language: "By virtue of language and only by virtue of language, world rules – beings
are."[46] Poetry fulfills this determination of the "essence of
language" in paradigmatic fashion. To the extent that poetry
is a particularly condensed linguistic phenomenon, it can take
up the role of collectively orienting us in the world: "Poetry
is the founding of being [*Sein*] in the word."[47]

In this interpretation of poetry, our point of departure seems
to be that, given that poetry is a linguistic phenomenon, it
must then be founded in language. In this way, we take poetry
to be an instantiation of a universal phenomenon. Yet Heidegger takes issue with this understanding. If poetry "is the
founding of being in the word," then poetry is that "whereby
everything first steps into the open, which we then discuss
and talk about in everyday language."[48] Poetry then precedes
language; it is "primordial language." Therefore, poetry is
not to be understood in terms of the "essence of language";

rather, it is the "essence of language" that is to be understood in terms of poetry. Poetry is the "essence of language."

For Heidegger, it is not simply the case that Hölderlin was the poet who best understood this conception of poetry. Rather, Hölderlin explicitly poetized the "essence of poetry."[49] In Hölderlin's poetry, a decision is made about poetry itself; in it, poetry as such appears in a new light. This is why Heidegger calls him the "poet's poet" – the "poet" who shows us what it means to be a poet, who also testifies to what it means to be a poet.

Poetry for Heidegger is not simply "primordial language" but also a "primordial language of a historical people."[50] With this thought, Heidegger steers his interpretation of Hölderlin in the direction of the "metapolitics 'of' the historical people." In a lecture from November of 1934 – during the time that he gave his lecture course on Hölderlin's hymns "Germania" and "The Rhine" – Heidegger characterized Hölderlin as the "most German of Germans."[51] The superlative is close to the philosopher because Hölderlin's poetry is the *unique* source out of which we are to experience what the "German" is and "who" the "Germans" are. Hölderlin is the poet who "founds" "history" for the "Germans"; he is the "founder of German beyng."[52]

In one of his first volumes of *Ponderings*, Heidegger is almost exclusively thinking of Hölderlin when he writes: "Only someone who is German can in an originarily new way poetize being and say being – he alone will conquer anew the essence of *theōria* and finally create *logic*."[53] Hölderlin legitimizes the singular role of the "Germans" in every respect. He is the one who supposedly laid the cornerstone of the "historical people." Already in the first 1934–5 lecture course on Hölderlin, Heidegger senses that this could be a problematic imposition on the poet. He claims that Hölderlin "has not yet become a force in the history of our people." Heidegger then adds, "Because he is not yet such a force, he must become such. In this process, we must keep in mind 'politics' in the highest and authentic sense, so much so that whoever accomplishes something here has no need to talk about the 'political.'"[54] The implicit jab at Carl Schmitt and his "concept of the political" is clear here.[55] However, it also became obvious that the "metapolitical" mission of Hölderlin's poetry – to say nothing of the fact that "metapolitics" might be just one of the motifs of his poetry – was doomed to fail. For the "people," Hitler was and would continue to be without a doubt the "most German of Germans."

Hölderlin's poetry provides key elements that help construct the narrative of the "history of being." Thus, at the end of the lecture course, Heidegger speaks of the "metaphysical locale of Hölderlin's poetizing."[56] This is the "middle of being itself." In order to place this "middle" in a "historical" situation, Heidegger interprets Hölderlin's first letter to his friend Casimir Ulrich Böhlendorff from December 4, 1801.[57] Heidegger cites the long and decisive passage from the letter where Hölderlin speaks of "what is authentically national," of the "*free* use of what is one's *own*" which is said to be "the most difficult." Hölderlin endows "us" and "the Greeks" with character attributes that are mutually related. "Clarity of exposition" is what is proper to "us," whereas "heavenly fire" is what defines "the Greeks." Thus, "with the exception of what must be the highest for the Greeks and for us – namely, the living relationship and destiny – we must not share anything identical with them." In fact, Hölderlin's description is concerned above all with the "regulation of art," yet Heidegger and many others have made it into a myth.

For Heidegger, Hölderlin's letter endorsed his plan to elaborate further what a preeminent significance the "Greeks" and the "Germans" had for European history, i.e., for the "history of being." Even though Heidegger does not refer to the "first" and "other inception" in the first lecture course on Hölderlin, it is nevertheless clear that his interpretation of Hölderlin's letter points in the same direction: "In fighting the battle of the Greeks, but on the reverse front, we become not Greeks, but Germans."[58] We must become German – by relating to the "Greeks" and the "first inception" – in order to let the "other inception" take place. In this transition, Hölderlin plays the primary role.[59]

In the first lecture course on Hölderlin, Heidegger cites the verse "Long is / The time, yet what is true / Comes to pass."[60] This is already an indication that the very "middle" of the "history of being" and "the event of appropriation" – which structures all the elements of Heidegger's narrative – originate in Hölderlin's hymn "Mnemosyne." In one of the *Black*

Notebooks from the early 1940s, Heidegger himself provides evidence to suggest that this claim is not entirely unfounded. After citing the aforementioned verse once more, he adds: "I have the feeling that another hundred years of neglect are needed before people start realizing what Hölderlin's poetry holds in store."[61]

At this point in his career, especially in *Contributions to Philosophy* – the most important attempt to think the "event of appropriation" in a "being-historical" manner – Heidegger had already, in his own way, grasped who Hölderlin was. There, the philosopher speaks of the "uniqueness of Hölderlin in the history of beyng": the "historical destiny of philosophy culminates in knowledge of the necessity to create a hearing for the words of Hölderlin." All this transcends the limits of "the 'scientific' and the 'literary-historiological.'" For Heidegger, the kernel of his interpretation of Hölderlin was the "question-worthiness of being."

Since Hölderlin is, in the "history of being," the poet of the "other inception" for Heidegger, he goes hand in hand with another Heideggerian project that is immanent to the "history of being." What we have in mind here is the aforementioned "overcoming of metaphysics." Here, the issue is no longer "to destroy Christian theology and western philosophy," as Heidegger had put it earlier. Rather, what is at stake in this "destructuring" of all underlying determinations of European philosophy is also a "historical" displacement, an "epochal" rupture which introduces the "other inception." In order to enable the "overcoming of metaphysics," the poet and thinker must collaborate, as it were. "Hölderlin's word" indeed prepares the "other inception of the history of beyng"; yet this "other inception" must first be decided in thinking "through the overcoming of metaphysics."[62] "This time," "thinking precedes poetizing."

Heidegger's late thinking distances itself from the crude movements of the "history of being." Around 1950, it is not simply the case that Heidegger's philosophy acquires a new style and tone; the arguments also take on a different importance. During this period, we find Heidegger reconsidering the notion of "machination," i.e., technology, to which he had devoted so much attention in the 1930s and 1940s. On the basis of certain problems that we still have to discuss,

Heidegger now thinks technology in a different way, namely, as "positionality." As was already the case with "machination," Heidegger's point of departure is that technology and science hold sway over the modern age. From this perspective, a verse from Hölderlin acquires a practically subversive aspect: "Full of merit / Yet poetically humans dwell upon this earth."[63] Humans who "dwell" are indeed "full of merit," that is to say, they dwell under the global conditions of technology, the economy, and the media network. And yet this "dwelling" is primarily "poetic." The "poetic" for Heidegger is the stance or attentiveness that is able to correspond to a "measure" in theory or in praxis. Poetry knows about human finitude and it is familiar with humanity's capabilities; it is aware of the possibility of tragic failure in the world. In the middle of World War II, this is the sense in which Heidegger refers to Sophocles' knowledge of the *polis* as expressed in the second choral ode of *Antigone*.[64] There, the tragedian describes the human as an "uncanny" living being who surpasses all others, who is unable to meet the "measure" and live communally in the *polis*.

As a whole, Heidegger's interpretation of Hölderlin was and continues to be rejected by Hölderlin scholarship and literary criticism.[65] As the reference to Norbert von Hellingrath indicates, this specific "political" reading can be historically situated in the reception of Hölderlin as belonging to the Stefan George "circle." Even though Heidegger states from the beginning that his philosophical intentions go far beyond any immediate application – such as any concrete political engagement – the fact that he links his interpretation of Hölderlin to the Third Reich is fatal. Having said this, from a philosophical point of view, Heidegger's interpretation of Hölderlin's poetry is quite singular. In a letter addressed to Heidegger, the literary critic Max Kommerell – highly respected by Heidegger – called his interpretation of Hölderlin "a sublime form of suicide."[66]

Philosophy and anti-Semitism

Already in a letter from 1916 to his wife Elfride, Heidegger speaks of a "Jewification [*Verjudung*] of our culture and universities."[67] This does not mean, of course, that Heidegger was interested in the "Jewish question" (as it was then called), if by "interest" we mean an increased attention to a given discourse. In the first decades of the twentieth century, the *ressentiment* against the conspicuous presence of Jews in cultural and educational sectors of German society was widespread, which is why it was possible for the National Socialists to capitalize on a general disposition with a heightened form of anti-Semitism.

Like many other German philosophers and poets – Schelling, Hölderlin, and Nietzsche, to name just a few – Heidegger came from a small provincial village where "Christian" prejudices against Jews were the order of the day. In a letter of 1920 to his wife Elfride, Heidegger writes: "Here there is a lot of talk of how many cattle now get bought up from the villages by the Jews [...] The farmers are gradually getting insolent up here too and everything is swamped with Jews and black marketeers."[68] This remark does not highlight religious prejudices. Instead, it evokes another anti-Semitic stereotype: Jews embody the soulless and calculating world of money and capitalism.

In his "Philosophical Autobiography," Karl Jaspers writes the following about Heidegger: "I spoke about the Jewish question and the evil non-sense of the Elders of Zion, to which he replied: 'There really is a dangerous international alliance of Jews.'"[69] After the fall of the German empire, the *ressentiment* against Jews increased. *The Protocols of the Elders of Zion* emerged in the context of the Dreyfus affair, which took place during the 1890s and penetrated the czarist politics of the time.[70] In this context, we come across anti-Semitic novels, as well as the increased importance of Zionism – which, especially since 1860, was a cause advocated by the Alliance Israélite Universelle and later, after 1897, by the Zionist World Organization. The latter's inaugural meeting in Basel became the fictional origin of the *Protocols*. The *Protocols* began to circulate widely after World War I, and they appeared in Germany for the first time in 1920.

Even from today's point of view, the impact of the *Protocols* was remarkable. Strictly speaking, they were a complete fiction rather than a forgery. The *Protocols* became the first source of modern anti-Semitism. Early on, Hitler was characterized as a "pupil of the Elders of Zion," supposedly because the *Protocols* encouraged him to develop a totalitarian racial politics.[71] Alfred Rosenberg commented on the *Protocols*. Hannah Arendt remarked that "the masses were not so frightened by Jewish world rule as they were interested in how it could be done, that the popularity of the *Protocols* was based on admiration and eagerness to learn rather than on hatred."[72] For Arendt, the methods of the National Socialists were obvious: "The Nazis started with the fiction of a conspiracy and modeled themselves, more or less consciously, after the example of the secret society of the Elders of Zion."[73] It was clear that the fall of the German empire and the "shameful peace" (*Schandfriede*) resulting from the Treaty of Versailles helped resurrect the phantasm of an international Jewish conspiracy, whose supposed goal was to destroy Germany. Heidegger, too, was held captive by this myth.

Though it is always a curious phenomenon when a philosopher gives in to common moods or general resentment in a non-critical manner, there is an important difference between these two levels, i.e., between non-critical reception of stereotypes and philosophical reflection. Heidegger's aforementioned three statements had long been familiar to Heidegger scholarship. They are without a doubt anti-Semitic, but in such a general way with respect to their historical context that they drew very little attention. However, for a philosopher who argues that "philosophy originates in the factical experience of life," the distinction between an unimportant private life caught up in everyday trivialities and a reflective philosophical existence is untenable.

Two other statements open onto a broader horizon. In another letter from 1920 to his wife Elfride, Heidegger complains about an interpretation of Hölderlin that remains unknown to us: "It is so grotesque one can only laugh – one wonders whether from this contamination we'll ever get back to the primordial freshness and rootedness of life again – sometimes one could really almost become a Spiritual anti-Semite."[74] From the perspective of a "spiritual anti-Semitism," that is, an anti-Semitism that clearly has no racial grounds, a Jewish "contamination" is contrasted to a "primordial freshness and rootedness of life." In view of the fact that Heidegger would later speak affirmatively of "spiritual

National Socialism," the concept of "spiritual anti-Semitism" is noteworthy.

Sometime around the turn of 1932–3, Hannah Arendt – Heidegger's highly gifted student and lover – asked Heidegger to comment on the "rumors" that he was supposedly an anti-Semite. Heidegger gave the following answer: "I am now just as much an anti-Semite in university issues as I was ten years ago in Marburg where, because of this anti-Semitism, I even earned Jacobsthal's and Friedländer's support."[75] This seems to be a carefully considered answer on Heidegger's part. It is less a confession of anti-Semitism in university issues than an appeal to the "support" of two Jews, the archeologist Paul Jacobsthal and the classical philologist Paul Friedländer, who was later a temporary prisoner at the Sachsenhausen concentration camp.

The *Black Notebooks* – the volumes of *Ponderings* that were written after 1938 and the *Observations* which go up to roughly 1948 – contain entries that displace Heidegger's anti-Semitism onto a different plane. The answer to the question of exactly which plane already entails an interpretative approach clarifying the kind of anti-Semitism we see in Heidegger. The question seems unnecessary, given that the real problematic is anti-Semitism in itself. I do not wish to dispute this. However, in philosophy, each thought must be understood in its own way. Judgments, be they political or moral, are never sufficient. This is why it is essential to consider Heidegger's anti-Semitic statements more closely.

All of Heidegger's anti-Semitic statements originate during the years of the persecution, deportation, and extermination of the Jews. Historically speaking, this is the period of the Nuremberg Racial Laws, the Night of the Broken Glass (*Reichspogromnacht*), the Wannsee Conference, and the subsequent systematic exterminations in Auschwitz, Birkenau, Treblinka, and so on. Heidegger was aware of the persecution and deportation of the Jews. It is difficult to say what exactly he knew or suspected concerning their extermination. As an influential professor of philosophy, he knew many former students who had become soldiers. His own sons fought on the Eastern front.

For Heidegger, in the age of "machination," nearly everything is reduced to an object of technological world domination. Whereas "Russians" and "Germans" prepare the

"other inception," other nations and cultures are in the
service of the "end" of history in the sense of a fundamental
"a-historicality."[76] In this narrative, Heidegger does not simply
equate National Socialism with Judaism; rather, Judaism is
said to be a forerunner of certain characteristics of National
Socialism. "*With their emphatically calculative giftedness*, the
Jews have for the longest time been 'living' in accord with the
principle of race, which is why they are also offering the most
vehement resistance to its unrestricted application."[77] National
Socialism – which institutionalized the "principle of race" – is
an epigone of Judaism, which followed this principle "for the
longest time," according to Heidegger.[78] That the Jews would
for this reason "offer the most vehement resistance to the
unrestricted application of this principle" is indeed a barely
comprehensible, if not infamous, statement. The superlative
"the most vehement" suggests a comparison. Yet with whom
or what? Over and beyond this, Heidegger leaves open what
the "unrestricted application" of the "race principle" might
mean. Does Heidegger have violence in mind? In comparison
to what was yet to happen, the Nuremberg Racial Laws may
very well be described as a "restricted application."

It is clear, however, that the Jewish and Nazi "institution
of racial breeding stems not from 'life' itself, but from the
overpowering of life by machination." "What machination
pursues with such planning is a *complete deracializing* of
peoples," which is at one with a "self-alienation of the peoples,"
i.e., the "loss of history." Heidegger is thus juxtaposing two
concepts of "race." One of these concepts is employed by
Jews and National Socialists alike in order to implement technological forms of breeding. For Heidegger, this results in the
loss of the other concept of race, namely, the understanding
of a "genuine" "race."[79] For the philosopher, a "genuine"
"race" in the sense of a natural, regional, and local lineage
remains a "necessary" condition of "historical Dasein."

It is precisely this lineage that Heidegger denies Judaism,
or, to be more precise, "World-Judaism." The latter takes up
the "world-historical task of uprooting all beings from being."[80]
In this way, the philosopher wants to establish that "the question of World-Judaism is not a racial" but a "metaphysical"
question. Regardless of the fact that Heidegger himself very
often suggests that the "race principle" and "metaphysics"

are by no means mutually exclusive, the assignment of a "world-historical task" to "World-Judaism" – a rhetoric that greatly resembles Hegel's philosophy of history – is of decisive importance. Insofar as "World-Judaism" – as Heidegger clearly does not doubt its existence – does not have any national or cultural traits, it is apparently predestined to represent "machination" and its "uprooting" effects on the theoretical and practical universalization of thought and life, which would then be in the service of the extinction of national identities. *The Protocols of the Elders of Zion* had argued that "World-Judaism" pursued this goal by means of a secret world conspiracy.

In 1942, the industrial mass extermination of Jews begins in Auschwitz; Heidegger composes the last notebook entries in which he speaks directly about Jews. "Jewry" (*Judenschaft*) – a word Martin Buber also uses – is "the principle of destruction within the epoch of the Christian West, i.e., metaphysics."[81] With this emblematic formulation, Heidegger adopts a phrase that resembles others in the history of anti-Semitism.[82] The "destruction" consists in the "overturning of the consummation of metaphysics in Hegel and Marx." Marx, the Jew, becomes the primary representative of the "principle of destruction." For, in Marxism, "spirit and culture become the 'superstructure' of life – i.e., of the economy, i.e., of the organization – of the biological – i.e., of the 'people.'" Heidegger again adopts the strategy of placing everything on the same rank, that is, of inverting the perpetrator–victim relationship as concerns the persecution, deportation, and extermination of the Jews. The "metaphysical" presuppositions of these events are then foisted on the Jews themselves. If the reasons that led to the persecution of the Jews are of a material nature – having to do with the economy, nation, and race – then the Jews are themselves responsible for their own persecution. For it was Marx who introduced such a "principle of destruction" into the "history of being."

Within the context of this interpretation of historical events, there emerges the most peculiar and disturbing thought that the extermination of the Jews was a kind of "self-extermination." Thus Heidegger identifies "what is essentially 'Jewish' in a metaphysical sense," i.e., the Marxist "principle of destruction," with "machination" pure and simple.[83] "Self-extermination" reaches a "climax in the history of being" when "what is essentially 'Jewish'" battles "against what is Jewish." This presupposes the totalization of what is "essentially 'Jewish'," namely, "machination." For it is only when this historical point is reached that every counter-movement to it can be grasped as "self-extermination." This notion of a totalization of what is "essentially 'Jewish'" *qua* "machination" is of course only possible against the backdrop of a perverse dramatization of factual history. Heidegger observes that "planetary war" is driven toward an event whose destruction is so absolute that it only has itself left to destroy. If it is possible to think this only on the basis of a mythological conception of the war, Heidegger's interpretation of the Shoah as the "self-extermination" of Judaism is, then, something other than a simple philosophical mistake. With this interpretation, Heidegger seems to be close to "consenting to horror."[84] Had Heidegger himself not spoken of the "necessity of affirming" National Socialism?

Amidst all his direct and indirect comments on the Jews, only once did Heidegger himself use the concept of "anti-Semitism." In a notebook entry from the end of the 1930s, Heidegger claims that "'prophecy' is a defensive technique against the destinal of history." "Prophecy" is an "instrument of the will of power." The "great prophets" are "Jews," "a mysterious fact which has not yet been thought." Then he adds the following parenthetical remark:

> Note for a jackass: this remark has nothing to do with "anti-Semitism." This is so foolish and so reprehensible, like the bloody – and, above all, the unbloody – actions of Christianity against "the heathens." That even Christianity denounces anti-Semitism as "un-Christian" belongs to the highly cultivated refinement of its power technique.[85]

Once again, Heidegger employs a figure of thought that appears throughout his anti-Semitic statements. Why does Heidegger come to speak about the problem or concept of "prophecy"? Is there a historical pretext for this? Hitler very often described himself as a "prophet" in his speeches, for example in the infamous Reichstag Speech of January 30, 1939 in which he announces the "annihilation of the Jewish race in Europe."[86] When Heidegger characterizes the "prophecy" as an "instrument of the will to power," he may very well have been thinking exclusively of this speech and Hitler's political staging. However, when he adds – Heidegger speaks in the present tense – that the "greatest prophets" are "Jews," it is Hitler who then turns into a "Jew," as it were. The words that announce the "annihilation of the Jewish race in Europe" are then attributed to a "Jew."

With a certain amount of fancy footwork, Heidegger tries to support the claim that this fatal configuration has nothing to do with anti-Semitism. He clearly seems to presume that anti-Semitism is primarily a Christian affair. Just as Christianity fought against the "heathens," it must apparently also go after the Jews. For Heidegger, the fact that many Christians nevertheless fiercely rejected the anti-Semitism of National Socialism was merely a "refinement of its [Christianity's] power technique." If anti-Semitism is supposed to be an exclusively Christian characteristic, then, admittedly, Heidegger's notebook entries cannot be qualified as anti-Semitic. However, in view of historical events such as the persecution, deportation, and extermination of the Jews, this reduction is simply absurd. By and large, Christianity did not motivate the anti-Semitism of the National Socialists.

In Heidegger's narrative of the "history of being," "World-Judaism" plays the role of the most important representative of "machination," i.e., of technology. "World-Judaism" is said to be capable of "completely uprooting all beings from being." In so doing, it embodies the "principle of destruction." The world of "uprooted beings" is the modern world, that is to say, a mobile and universal lifestyle that not only neglects but indeed destroys the possibility of simple relations in the life and "home" of a community. The "Jew" represents this mobile universal way of life that is then linked to the "power of capital" – a stereotype of modern anti-Semitism typified in *The Protocols of the Elders of Zion*.

The question here is how these ideas relate to Heidegger's philosophy as a whole. We know that their publication caused many to demand that Heideggerian thought be banned or expelled from philosophy (see chapter 5, "Reverberations"). This thought is considered to be the "introduction of National Socialism into philosophy."[87] The problem, however, is not so simple.

Even though Heidegger's "philosophical" notes on the Jews are almost nowhere to be found outside the *Black Notebooks* – the importance of which Heidegger greatly esteemed – it is not possible to limit the problem to these texts alone. They are indeed deeply inscribed in the narrative of the "history of being." However, this does not mean that we can search for and identify the essence of Heidegger's anti-Semitic statements in every Heidegger text. Why? The French philosopher Paul Ricoeur once spoke, in a somewhat different context, of a "hermeneutics of suspicion."[88] According to this hermeneutics, texts are determined by presuppositions that do not appear in the text itself. For Ricoeur, Heidegger is himself an interpreter who exposes how philosophical texts have, unbeknownst to their authors, fallen prey to "metaphysics." This does not mean, of course, that this hermeneutics yields no interesting results. On the contrary: Heidegger's reading of European philosophy as a metaphysical thinking which "has forgotten being" understands itself as one possible vision of this philosophy. However, Heidegger's thought will never abandon precisely this status of a merely possible interpretation. In this sense, it is entirely possible to interpret *Being and Time* against the backdrop of the history of anti-Semitism and Heidegger's entanglement in it. Nevertheless, we may not with any certainty claim that *Being and Time* is as anti-Semitic a work as Hitler's *Mein Kampf*.

Thus we may *not* transfer Heidegger's statements concerning "World-Judaism" – especially in the *Black Notebooks* – onto his thinking as a whole. Yet these statements are bound to arouse a "suspicion" that will trouble anyone dealing with Heidegger. His philosophy goes astray along horrifying, wayward paths that belong to the movement of this thinking. Whoever believes he can encounter this thinking without also pursuing these wayward paths will never be able to develop an interpretation worth considering.

On the structure of the "event of appropriation"

The event of appropriation appropriates.[89]

We can say, in short, that the question of the "meaning of being" as an explication of Dasein's "temporality" and "historicity" persisted through all the political and ideological developments of the beginning of the 1930s. In and through a movement we tend to oversimplify by calling it "the turn," the constellation of these essential concepts was transformed. *Being and Time*'s "analytic of Dasein" became a "thinking of being" that no longer considered "Dasein's historicity" but instead the "history of being." However, Heidegger did not envision the "history of being" in an abstract way, as if it were the theory of a given understanding of history; rather, the "history of being" is itself in direct contact with a history that happens factically. The notion of a "history of being" is itself only possible at a given point in history when this very history gives rise to the knowledge of itself.[90] The "thinking of being" is itself a necessary element in the "history of being." The central concept that this movement of thought is supposed to articulate is the "event of appropriation" (*Ereignis*).

Contributions to Philosophy (*Of the Event*) – first published only in 1989 – lays out the change in the most important conceptual matrix in Heidegger's thinking with respect to *Being and Time*. Most Heidegger scholars and readers judge this text to be Heidegger's "second major work." In this work, we can see the path (or paths) along which Heidegger's thinking must travel after *Being and Time* in order to come to a modified project of this kind.

To put it roughly, *Contributions to Philosophy* no longer takes on the question of the "meaning of being" – or the "meaning of beyng" as Heidegger now calls it – by passing through an "analysis" of Dasein. The claim now is "to think beyng in its essential occurrence without taking beings as the point of departure," i.e., without taking the "exceptional being," i.e., Dasein, as a springboard for the actual problematic of "being."[91] Such a thinking, which Heidegger calls an "inventive thinking (*Er-denken*) of beyng," has the character of an "attempt" that is all too easily misunderstood if interpreted as a "doctrine."[92] We miss the extraordinary nature of this thinking if our goal is to extract dogmatic theses from the *Contributions to Philosophy*. Nevertheless, this work is not at all a mere experiment devoid of any particular intention.

In *Being and Time*, the basic structure of "fundamental ontology" is the "ontological difference" between "being" and "beings." It delineates the two poles between which the question of the "meaning of being" oscillates. Its point of departure is a reciprocal grounding. "Being" must "always already" be understood in order for "beings" to be known. "Beings" must be considered as such in order for the "meaning of being" to be explicated. It would be possible to reflect on the "meaning of being" in order to explain "beings." Yet Heidegger recognizes that such a "reversal" does not accomplish the actual goal of investigating "being itself." A mere "reversal" of the "ontological difference" is still stuck in a schema that, however justified it be, blocks access to the decisive path toward "beyng."

In *Contributions to Philosophy*, as Heidegger now looks for an entirely different "project" of thought, he emphatically claims to "bring this questioning altogether outside of that difference between being and beings." This is the reason why "being is now written as beyng," which is "supposed to indicate that being is here no longer thought metaphysically."[93] "Metaphysics" is the "name" Heidegger uses "conditionally" to "characterize the entire previous history of philosophy."[94] Within this unthought schema, i.e., the "distinction between beings and being," "metaphysics" is only ever able to think "being" as the general essence of "beings," that is to say, as an a priori or as being-ness. *Contributions to Philosophy* is supposed to articulate "beyng" in language in a different way.

An essential modification in Heidegger's thinking post-*Being and Time* is captured in the succinct and recurrent formulation, "the question of being is the question of the truth of beyng."[95] In *Being and Time*, Heidegger was already able to show how the traditional understanding of truth as the logical adequation or correspondence between thought and things presupposes – and at the same time forgets – a more original understanding of truth. The possibility of making true or false statements about "beings" presupposes that "beings" be able to appear in the first place. The Greek word for truth, *alētheia*, which Heidegger translates more or less literally as "unconcealment," harbors this possibility. Solely on the basis of a privileging of "logic," traditional "metaphysical" thinking grasps truth as propositional veracity without realizing how this notion ultimately rests on an understanding of truth as "unconcealment." The "question of the truth of beyng" that is raised in *Contributions to Philosophy* does not grasp truth as "propositional truth" but, rather, originally as the ontological happening of truth itself. Understood in this way, it is possible to identify "truth" with "beyng": "The essence of truth resides in its essential occurrence as what is true of beyng and thus in its becoming the origin of the sheltering of what is true in beings, whereby these latter first become beings."[96] Heidegger does not take "truth" to be a criterion for making true or false judgments. Rather, "truth" has an origin in "beyng" itself. It "essences" and, in this "essencing," it becomes the origin of "what is true," i.e., of "beings," which can then attest to their origins in "beyng."

In *Being and Time*, Heidegger uses the term "clearing" (*Lichtung*) to describe Dasein because the latter is marked by a "disclosedness" in which it itself and other beings become transparent and "accessible in the light."[97] Starting with the 1930 lecture titled "On the Essence of Truth," this idea becomes displaced into the notion that the "clearing" is actually truth itself, i.e., unconcealment (*alētheia*). In *Contributions to Philosophy*, Heidegger asks us to bear in mind that the "truth of being" is no longer simply "the sublation of the concealed, i.e., its liberation and transformation into unconcealment. It instead means precisely the grounding of the abyssal ground for the *concealment* (the hesitant withholding)."[98] The concept of the "truth of being" as the "clearing of the concealment" makes it possible to grasp, in the "essence" or "essential occurrence of truth," "precisely" the concealments and distortions that cannot be understood as characteristics of beings but rather of "beyng."

It is important to understand why Heidegger so insists on the dimension of "concealment" in his understanding of truth. Everything that appears never fully shows itself. The most ordinary things are a direct proof of this. Take the objects of perception, for example: initially, we only see the side facing us. The back or inside of a closed closet evades our perception. Husserl characterized this phenomenon as "adumbration." However, in his explication of "concealment," Heidegger goes beyond this trait pertaining to the appearing of things. It is not simply that parts of things or "beings" escape our perception; rather, what is at stake in "concealment" is the withdrawal of the very dimension in which "beings" appear. The "clearing" that lets "beings" appear is precisely what "conceals" itself. In terms of both the things that appear and the dimension in which they appear, the "clearing" always entails a "concealment." Nevertheless, to the extent that we must understand, as it were, the "whole truth," we may not unilaterally grasp truth only as a "clearing" but rather as the "clearing of concealment," that is to say, as a possibility of knowledge constituted by the limits of knowledge. In other words, a thinking that adheres only to the self-showing of "beings" and does not take into account their origin, i.e., "being" – which does not show itself – can never be in accordance with the "truth of beyng."

Contributions to Philosophy presents us with the related thought that, because of this interaction between appearing and concealing in the "clearing of concealment," the "truth of beyng" can itself be concealed, giving rise to historical epochs that are marked by the loss of "beyng," i.e., by the "abandonment by beyng." Thus Heidegger writes at one point, "This truth of beyng is indeed nothing distinct from beyng but rather is the most proper essence of beyng. Therefore, it depends on the history of beyng as to whether beyng bestows or refuses this truth and itself and thus genuinely brings into its history for the first time the abyssal."[99] This "refusal" of "truth" must not be understood in the sense of a deficit if we are to understand Contributions to Philosophy. This "hesitant withholding" is a positive character of "beyng" that historically enables, in an abyssal way, the wayward and errant paths of human beings. After all, were human beings always to grasp everything purely and simply, we would not be able to explain how the history of mankind can take such catastrophic turns.

In Contributions to Philosophy, Heidegger thus philosophizes in the context of a "fundamental experience" according to which the "refusal" of "beyng" has become manifest as the exclusive privilege of "beings," i.e., of objects and their instrumental use. At stake here is the integrity of the relation between "beyng" and "beings." Every single thing, whether natural or man-made, is evaluated solely from the point of view of its availability and use. The human behaves merely as a "technologized animal."[100] Given that in this "essential occurrence of beyng," all "beings" are understood within the horizon of "making" (Machen) and "producibility" (Machbarkeit), the philosopher describes this "occurrence" as "machination" (*Machenschaft*). The intention of an "inventive thinking of beyng" consists in illuminating this desolate relation with "beings" so as to take a stance against it. The "task" that remains is to enable the *"retrieval of beings out of the truth of beyng,"* that is to say, to oppose philosophically the way humans destructively relate to things and themselves.[101] According to Heidegger, such an act of resistance cannot result in "utopic" recipes that prescribe how to make the world a better place; rather, the point initially is to let the "refusal" of "beyng" as such come to language for once, so as to become something we "can experience." Without being completely reducible to it, the actuality of the National Socialist state plays a role in this historical diagnosis. As National Socialism began making technological and economic reforms in Germany, Heidegger began to consider National Socialism – and, in an absurd manner, "World-Judaism" – to be a representative of "machination."

Heidegger has characterized this "basic experience" of "history" – the fact that the world is ever more out of joint – as "plight." "Plight" (*Not*) is a state in which something is used while remaining "refused." If we turned to the concepts of *Being and Time*, we could explain "plight" as a "way of being" of Dasein. By contrast, the way human beings currently comport themselves appears to "lack the sense of plight" for Heidegger. This attitude bears itself out as the "unbroken supply of useful and enjoyable things, things already objectively present, ones which can be increased through progress."[102] An everyday "lack of plight" masks the "compulsion" (*Nötigung*) which stems from the "refusal" of the "truth of beyng." Given that this "lack of plight" avoids every thought that does not fall under the sway of what is "present-at-hand," this saturated situation is itself to be understood as "plight." For those who wish to think past the established conditions of the present and of political society, it is a matter of experiencing *"the lack of a sense of plight in the midst of this plight,"* its "breakthrough."[103] Therefore, we must meditate the "plight of this lack of plight" as the "compulsion," i.e., that which the present "refuses." When human beings understand what the subterranean and ongoing totalization of technocratic tendencies "refuses" them, "terror" seizes them; in and through this "terror," "plight" lets the possibility of the "other inception" strike like a lightning bolt. In this sense, "plight" is one of the first driving forces of Heideggerian thought.

In this era of "machination," Dasein – or "*Da-sein*," as Heidegger writes more often during this period – acquires a particular determination. We already indicated that, in *Being and Time*, Dasein is not simply identical to the human being but is rather the most original possibility of the being of the human. In *Contributions to Philosophy*, the "history of being" sharpens the distinction between the "human" and Dasein. "*Animal rationale*" is the traditional – and for Heidegger, that always means "metaphysical" – determination of the "human being" as a living being. Since Plato and Aristotle, the great philosophers have interpreted the human as a being that stands between the sensuous and the supersensuous. Like animals, the human has a body with sensuous needs; unlike animals, it has "language" or "reason" (*logos*) by means of which it turns toward the supersensuous or "ideas." Thus Aristotle determines the human being as the animal that has language (*zōon logon echon*). This interpretation was reinforced in the modern age starting with the Cartesian dualism between substances, i.e., between "thinking" (*res cogitans*) and "extension" (*res extensa*). Heidegger, however, opposes "*Da-sein*" to this determination of the human being as a "rational animal."

Heidegger does not see this opposition as being his own personal insight. Rather, his view is that history announces this "transformation" of the "rational animal" into "*Da-sein*." In the "refusal" proper to the "truth of beyng," the possibility of such a "transformation" shows itself of its own accord. What's more, this "refusal" appears as a kind of mission or "task" to "ground" "*Da-sein*."[104] The notion of the "transformation" of the "rational animal" into "*Da-sein*" shows how Heidegger's thinking belongs to the European tradition which has, since Plato, conceived of the "human being" as a "being" yet to be formed (*bildendes*). Another future "human" is always supposed to overcome the previous "human" such as he is. At the heart of European thought, there is a "revolutionary" conception of the "human." The "human" is the animal that always has to be "educated" (*gebildet*).

The notion of a "grounding" of "*Da-sein*" makes it clear that we may not understand Dasein either as a thing present-at-hand or as a possibility of being that is "always already" available. Even though the concept of "grounding" suggests a voluntary action on Dasein's part, Heidegger understands it differently. The "refusal" of the "truth of beyng" "assigns" or "accords" a "grounding" to Dasein. Accordingly, just as *Da-sein* can, on the one hand, ground itself, on the other hand this "grounding" is given to it. For Heidegger, the "grounding" of *Da-sein* is thus a "compliance."[105] Here we can see a singular and fundamental movement of Heidegger's thinking that remains relevant for us today. The philosopher no longer considers *"Da-sein"*'s possibility of action to be the subjective faculty of a self-contained "spontaneity"; rather, this possibility is interpreted as the relation between a call and an answer. It is then possible to describe this fundamental movement of Heidegger's thought as "responsive."[106] The elements of his thinking can no longer be understood as isolated from one another but, instead, only in terms of a "re-lation" (*Ver-hältnis*).[107] Each singular movement of one of these elements "corresponds" to another. Each movement "needs" another movement from out of which – and toward which – it can take place.

Heidegger calls the happening of the "refusal" of the "truth of beyng" – and the resulting possibility of a "rapture at the truth of beyng" – the "event of appropriation" (*Ereignis*). Among the many meanings of this word, the sense of *Eigenen* (proper) and its corresponding verb *eignen* (to be proper for) certainly play the primary role, though not the only one. For Heidegger, the word *Ereignis* is a *singulare tantum*, that is to say, it is used only in the singular on account of its "singularity." Whereas it commonly shows up in everyday language in the reflexive form of *sich ereignen* (to happen), Heidegger understands this word transitively: the *Ereignis ereignet*, the "event of appropriation appropriates."[108] The question then is: what does the event appropriate? The answer: it appropriates the human being into *"Da-sein."*

Heidegger conceives of the "transformation" of humans into *"Da-sein"* as a "coming into one's own." In order to grasp the structure of this happening, we must not understand the "event of appropriation" and that which is "appropriated" as an object that a subject dons, as it were. The "event of appropriation" – or "beyng," as Heidegger also calls it – consists in the interaction between two elements that become what they "truly" are only in and through this interaction.

The movement of this interaction shows up again in the basic structure of reciprocal "need." In the "fundamental experience" of "plight," which Heidegger refers to as "refusal" but also as "hesitant withholding," an appeal or initial "call" is made to the human being who responds to it. In "plight," the human being is accorded what he "needs" in order to transform "plight." The self-differentiated unity of the "event of appropriation" emerges only when one of these elements relates to the other.

The central point and axis of this reciprocity is the "turning."[109] In the peculiar and occasionally awkward language of *Contributions to Philosophy*, this is articulated as follows: "What is this originary turning in the event? Only the intrusion of beyng, as the appropriation of the 'there,' brings '*Da-sein*' to itself and thus to the carrying out (sheltering) of the steadfastly grounded truth in beings, which find their abode in the cleared concealment of the 'there.'"[110]

The "responsive" structure – "turning" is Heidegger's term – of the "event of appropriation" consists in the fact that the "truth of beyng" brings and "ap-propriates" (*er-eignet*) "*Da-sein*" to itself; conversely and simultaneously, this allows for the "truth of beyng" to come and be "ap-propriated" (*er-eignet*) to its there (*Da*). "*Da-sein*" responds to the "event of appropriation" which in turn becomes the event that it is only by means of Dasein's response. Heidegger characterizes this inner movement of the "event of appropriation" as the "*oscillation of needing and belonging.*"[111]

This "turn" in the "responsive" structure of the relationship between "*Da-sein*" and "beyng" has often been described as a pivotal moment in Heidegger's thinking, leading many to speak of this thinking in terms of a "before" or "after" the "turn." It is certainly the case that Heidegger's thinking undergoes a restructuring after *Being and Time*. However, to identify this modification exclusively with the "turn" misses the point. Heidegger's philosophy is not a thinking situated "before" or "after" the turn but rather "in" the turn. It is always interested in the moment when something – "existence," "history," "truth," "world," etc. – effects a turning. Amidst these revolutions and reversals, we also find abrupt ruptures that Heidegger nevertheless tried to conceal, as is the case, for example, with his wayward political path.

The difficulty and ambiguity of Heidegger's "event of appropriation" lies in the question of how much importance we should grant the "negative" aspect of this organizing figure in the "history of being." Does the "event of appropriation" entail a transposition of the "history of being" into an "authentic" state of "one's own," a state that, by means of the "factical" occurrence of the "truth of beyng," abandons the corruption and alienation of modernity? If so, this would be an occurrence framed theologically, similar to the Christian notion of Parousia, i.e., the Second Coming of Christ. Or, alternatively, do the "hesitant withholding" and the "refusal" of the "truth of beyng" constitute the essential characteristics of the "event of appropriation" to such an extent that the "openness" of this event is to be thought not as a "purity of being" but as a "freedom" that presupposes the "negative"?[112] In this sense, this occurrence might represent a new way of describing, for example, the narrative of historical processes or revolutions.

Furthermore, we would have to return to the question we have neglected thus far, namely, the question of the relationship between the "other inception" and the "event of appropriation."[113] In this way, the latter gets inevitably entangled in the context of that "metapolitics" which Heidegger tried to develop in 1933 as his answer to the "National Revolution." And even if the notion or figure of the "other inception" could be dissociated from this context, we would still have to analyze it again from the point of view of its revolutionary and philosophical ambitions. Can there be something like "another inception," pure and simple? Has not each "inception" "always already" happened before one can even recognize it as such? Or, to put the question differently, is the "inception" not "always already" a "response"?

Art and the "struggle between world and earth"

Heidegger's lecture from the mid-1930s titled "The Origin of the Work of Art" ends enigmatically with the following

Hölderlin verses: "Reluctant to leave the place / Is that which dwells near the origin."[114] Earlier, Heidegger had defined art as "the setting-itself-to-work of truth," that is, as a "sheltering" of "truth" in the "work" where "truth" functions "as both subject and object of the setting."[115] This "setting-itself-to-work of truth" always had to be understood as an "inception." It is clear that the last part of the lecture belongs to the "metapolitics 'of' the historical people." On the other hand, Heidegger announces here an understanding of art that he would continue to pursue up through the last stage of his thinking.

In 1969, Heidegger writes that "sculpture would be the embodiment of places. Places, in preserving and opening a region, hold something free gathered around them."[116] More than thirty years earlier, in "The Origin of the Work of Art," Heidegger had described "a Greek temple," as well as a Van Gogh painting featuring "peasant shoes."[117] What if the "temple" or the "peasant shoes" "embodied places" in which "truth sets itself to work"? What if both "temple" and "peasant shoes," each in their own way, went beyond the "metapolitics 'of' the historical people" and presented us with an "origin" or "inception"?

For Heidegger, the artwork is a "place" in a very specific manner. In the later developments of *Space and Art*, "sculpture," i.e., the sculpted body, is said to delimit a "region" in which we can experience "something free." Here it is also possible to understand "region" and this "something free" as "earth" and "world." This is indeed the case in the lecture on "The Origin of the Work of Art," where the artwork appears as the "struggle of world and earth."[118]

According to Heidegger's *Being and Time*, "being-in-the-world" is one of Dasein's most important "existential determinations." "Dasein tends to understand its own being in terms of the beings to which it is essentially, continually, and most closely related," i.e., the "world."[119] Given that Dasein has this tendency, it becomes necessary for "fundamental ontology" to introduce the "ontological concept" of the "worldliness of the world in general" which co-founds Dasein.[120] This "existential" carries a particular "multiplicity of meanings" that can be broken down into four different concepts of "world." The first concept contains the ontic, that is to say, material determination of "world," as "the totality of beings which can be objectively present within the world." The second provides the "ontological" determination of "world" as the "name of a region which embraces a multiplicity of beings." The third concept of world interprets the world as "that '*in which*' a factical Dasein 'lives' as Dasein." Finally, the fourth conceptualizes "world" as "worldliness." In accordance with *Being and Time*'s intention to analyze the "worldliness of the world in general," the third concept of "world" is the one that is most explicitly thematized. When that is not the case, the investigation is guided by the first concept of world.

The milieu, "'*in which*' a factical Dasein 'lives,'" is the "surrounding world."[121] In this "surrounding world," Dasein is concerned with "taking care" of "useful things."[122] An "in order to" characterizes each "useful thing." Using a "useful thing" always "in order to ..." implies a "reference." Examined more closely, this "reference" turns out to be the "relevance" of "useful things."[123] "Relevance" is the "what-for of service-ability and the wherefore of usability." The "what-for" and the "wherefore" make up the nexus of a "totality of relevance." We discover a given "relevance" in advance always in terms of a "totality of relevance." The fact that Dasein "always already" finds and orients itself in such a "totality" is an indication that this "totality contains an ontological relation to world."[124] The "totality of significance" that is given in advance seems to determine not just "useful things" but every "being." Thus Heidegger can write: "*As that for which one lets beings be encountered in the kind of being of relevance, the wherein of self-referential understanding is the phenomenon of world.*"[125] In *Being and Time*, Heidegger has no doubt taken "useful things" and their integration into a "totality of relevance" as *the* paradigm for understanding "beings" pure and simple.[126] However, it later became clear to him that the analysis of the "worldliness of the world" that starts from "useful things" presupposed a preliminary methodological decision – namely that Dasein must be initially analyzed in terms of its "everydayness" – that influenced the way in which an understanding of "world" could unfold.

In the early 1930s, within the context of a radical restructuring of Heidegger's thought, this preliminary decision underwent a modification that produced ambivalent results. Possibly influenced by the National Socialist ideology of "blood and soil" – which Hölderlin's poetry made sublime – Heidegger recognizes that Dasein also lives on the "earth" and not just in the "world." He characterizes the "earth" as a "power" that relates to "world" in the "struggle of world and earth."[127] On the one hand, it is possible that Heidegger came to this idea because of his understanding of "truth as the primal struggle between clearing and concealment."[128] On the other hand, he may also have been led to it by the Heraclitean notion of *polemos*, according to which a "battle" or "struggle" organizes the relations between gods and humans, slaves and free men.[129] Heidegger is trying, on the one hand, to phenomenologically justify the decision to thematize "world" as the earth's counterpart; on the other hand, the "earth" belongs to the *mythical*, i.e., narrative dimension of the "metapolitics 'of' the historical people." All things considered, the figure of a "struggle between world and earth" is tied to the conspicuous Heideggerian tendency to think *relationally*.

As Heidegger puts it in "The Origin of the Work of Art," "world" is the "self-opening openness of the broad paths of the simple and essential decisions in the destiny of a historical people."[130] "Earth" is the "unforced coming forth of the continually self-closing, and in that way, self-sheltering." "World" is the "openness" in which the earth's coming forth can unfold itself. "Earth" is the "sheltering" on the basis of which "world" can be founded.

There is a striking movement at work in this relation between "world" and "earth." The "earth" presses into the "open": plants grow, their roots reach deep into the "earth." The "world" that offers a space for praxis and poiesis "needs" a foundation it can rely on and "build" upon. The resulting movement is a reciprocal interpenetration, a "reciprocity." This can be taken in two senses: on the one hand, in order to unfold in opposite directions, "earth" and "world" "need" each other. On the other hand, each delimits and excludes the other. The "self-closing" does not permit an "openness"; it would like to cancel out the "openness" which, as it were, seeks to escape the "self-closing" – which tries to expand itself in the growing of plants, for example. From this perspective, the "reciprocity" between "earth" and "world" is a "struggle." Heidegger considers this "struggle" to be a characteristic of the "truth of beyng." For the "struggle between world and earth" only happens if "truth" takes place as "the primal struggle between clearing and concealment." Thus the "struggle between world and earth" is actually the "primal struggle between clearing and concealment."

Hölderlin's poetry played a role in shaping Heidegger's concept of "earth." Already in the first lecture course on Hölderlin from the winter semester of 1934–5, Heidegger cites a verse that is attributed to Hölderlin, although no original manuscript of the poem exists. "Full of merit, yet poetically / Humans upon this earth."[131] Almost two decades later, Heidegger will again undertake an interpretation of this verse, which is of major importance for understanding his philosophy.[132]

"Earth" here does not, of course, refer to the globe but rather to the specific "place" of an "origin," i.e., the "homeland."[133] It is the "earth of the homeland." Throughout his thinking as a whole – and not simply in the context of his "metapolitics" – Heidegger thus advocates for an anti-universalism which, in the age of the universalizing projects of technology, science, capital, and mainstream media, is extremely problematic. What do we make of the fact that "being itself" clearly dwells in the middle of a regional "history" that is related to a specific "earth"?[134] Indeed, on the heels of a "metapolitical" radical-ization, wouldn't it be possible to think that the concept of "earth" does not at all signify a common (metaphysical) genus of different "earths"? That, instead, Heidegger grants only the Germans the possibility of living in a "struggle between earth and world"? On the other hand, in a time marked by massive migration flows, we must summon a specific under-standing of "origin" if we are to grasp why "flight" is even a problem. In a living space (*Lebensraum*) "always already" understood as universal, this is hardly possible.

In *Contributions to Philosophy*, Heidegger comes back to the notion of a "struggle between world and earth." In the "event of appropriation," Dasein is the "fulcrum" of the "turning." This "turning acquires its truth only if it is carried out as the struggle between earth and world, such that what is true is sheltered in beings."[135] The task of "art" is precisely to "shelter what is true in beings."[136] At the same time, Hei-degger also asks: "Why is the earth silent at this destruction?

Because the earth is not allowed the struggle with a world, not allowed the truth of beyng."[137] In the epoch of the "abandonment by being," the "truth of beyng" remains "silent." As "nature," "earth" is "separated out from beings by the natural sciences." "What was nature once?" asks Heidegger; he answers by returning to the myth of the "Greeks": "It was the site of the moment of the advent and sojourning of the gods." Now, nature is "completely set out in the compulsion of calculative machination and economics." As a consequence, the "struggle between world and earth" can no longer happen. This is Heidegger's way of saying that "art has to come to an end – indeed must be at an end."[138]

However, this is just one of the many branches that characterize the path-like character of Heidegger's thought. In the context of the problem of "overcoming metaphysics," the philosopher speaks of "overcoming aesthetics."[139] The latter ought to enable an understanding of "art" that goes beyond Kantian and Nietzschean "aesthetics." From this point of view, Heidegger thinks of the "moment of a history without art," which "can be more historical and more creative than eras of widespread bustle over art."[140] However, within the "history of being," this thought also presupposes that it was once possible for the "originary necessity of the essence of art" to make itself necessary "on the basis of a need" and "bring the truth of beyng into decision." In the "metapolitical" context of the lecture "The Origin of the Work of Art," Heidegger still, perhaps, held onto this hope.

"Overcoming metaphysics"

Nearly twenty-five years ago, Jürgen Habermas compared our "current situation" with "that of the first generation of Hegel's disciples": "At the time the basic condition of philosophizing changed; since then, there has been no alternative to post-metaphysical thinking."[141] Today, (almost) every philosopher shares this view. Habermas is here thinking of the so-called "Hegelians of the left," Karl Marx being one example. Taking Hegel's thought to be the limit of a metaphysical understanding of philosophy, Heidegger is one of the philosophers who engages with Hegel's interpretation of his own thought as the end of philosophy pure and simple. Thus hardly any other philosopher in the twentieth century has insisted as much as Heidegger on the project of "overcoming metaphysics."

In his early lecture courses as well as in *Being and Time*, Heidegger speaks of the task of carrying out a phenomenologico-hermeneutical "destructuring [*Destruktion*] of the history of ontology."[142] This "destructuring" implies going through the long history of commentary and interpretation of "ontological concepts" in order to come back to the "original experiences" that gave rise to these concepts.[143] This "destructuring" does not have the "*negative* sense of disburdening ourselves from the ontological tradition."[144] The "destroying" is not the same as breaking a stone to pieces with a hammer – something which, incidentally, Nietzsche's "philosophizing with a hammer" also *isn't*; rather, it is similar to shaking a pan of gold in order to let the gold at the bottom become more and more visible as the obscuring matter is sifted from it. However, a "negative sense" is in play here. In a destructive way, the "destructuring" aims at the "dominant way we treat the history of ontology." It calls this ontology into question. If it is philosophically necessary to come back to the original sense of "ontological concepts," this is because current concepts have proven insufficient, to the extent that they may be lifeless or dead.

The "destructuring of the history of philosophy" does not make the history of philosophy disappear. On the contrary, it has the decisive role of laying bare for once the history of fundamental texts and their interpretations. With the notion of "destructuring," Heidegger presents philosophy with an inexhaustible horizon of hermeneutical projects. The hermeneutical philosophy of someone like Hans-Georg Gadamer draws extensively on Heidegger's program and its execution. The enterprise of Derridean "deconstruction," too, is linked to Heidegger's thought.

In his 1934 summer semester lecture course titled "Logic as the Question of the Essence of Language," Heidegger speaks of "the fundamental task of shaking up this logic from top to bottom." Initially, he concedes that this "shaking up," which he had "been working on for ten years," is "grounded on a transformation of our Dasein itself."[145] One year later, in the lecture course "Introduction to Metaphysics," Heidegger again emphasizes his wish to "unhinge logic from its *ground* up."[146] Thus in the middle of the 1930s he picks up on the "destruction of the history of ontology" and links it to the program of his "metapolitics." The "transformation of our Dasein" recalls the "national revolution" that Heidegger supported. If thought was bound to change, so too was "logic."

We can sketch this "shaking up" as follows: "logic" is the "science of *logos*." The Aristotelian conception of *logos* as *logos apophantikos* exhibits and expresses "how a thing is and what the matter is."[147] The logos is a "propositional statement" about "beings." We make statements not only in the narrow sense of saying a sentence out loud; we also make statements when we *think*. Thought can be either true or false, according to the statement's truth or falsity. Certain axioms or laws of thought stipulate whether a thinking is true or false. "Logic" exists for us to know right thinking from wrong. Thus, as the "science of *logos*," "logic" is initially the "exhibition of the formal structure of thinking" and the "exposition of its rules."[148]

"Logic" "dissects" thinking into the "basic elements" of the propositional statement. In addition, it indicates how several of these "basic elements" are to be "woven" and "put together" for the statement to be valid. It shows us the requirements for making inferences and judgments correctly. For Heidegger, the three most important axioms are the principles of identity, non-contradiction, and reason.[149]

Logic as a philosophical science, however, is not the whole of philosophy. Very early on, starting with Xenophon (396–314 BCE), the director of Plato's Academy, logic is accompanied by two other sciences. Philosophy as a whole is divided into the classical disciplines of logic, ethics, and physics.[150] It is important to note that *thinking* necessarily has to happen both in the field of ethics and in the natural sciences. It thus follows that logic has pride of place, as it reflects on the kind of deliberation (justifying, criticizing, regulating, releasing, etc.) that accompanies every human activity.

Yet this does not exhaust the meaning of what we understand logic to be. In the everyday world, we find "phrases" that transfer the scientific understanding of logic, not unjustifiably, onto everyday occurrences. Thus we take something "consequential" to be "logical." We do not mean this in the sense of "science of *logos*," but "rather we mean the inner consequentiality of an issue, situation or process."[151] In everyday speech, this "consequentiality" is a mode of scientific logic that has been downgraded into the ordinary. The "undifferentiated and habitual form of the propositional sentence: a is b" is a "fundamental trait of everyday Dasein" with respect to "its undifferentiated comportment towards beings precisely as something present at hand."[152] Conversely, scientific logic is – or wishes to be – an explicit formalization of everyday speech acts. Logic formalizes the intrinsically formal "consequentiality" of an acting Dasein.

There is thus a link between the "logic of things and the logic of thinking." Thinking and things are "turned towards each another," "each turns again into the other," "each claims the other."[153] In the context of a human world order oriented toward "reason," this "being-turned-toward-each-other" between thinking and things, "logic" and "ontology," goes without saying. "Reason," as a "being-turned-toward-each-other" of thoughts and things, retains its status as the norm, even as our passions seemingly make a mess of the world. According to Hegel, a "cunning of reason" guides even the most painful of actions in a world-historical context.[154] The "being-turned-toward-each-other" of thoughts and things is the condition that makes it possible for *"what is rational to be actual [...] and for what is actual to be rational."*[155]

It goes without saying that a "destabilization of logic" – as Heidegger also puts it later on – has to "destabilize the human being."[156] When the axioms of thought and speech are up for debate, this affects our interpretation of ourselves. If, as Heidegger tells us time after time, the human being is metaphysically determined as the *animal rationale*, and if the sense of *ratio* as *logos* is "destroyed," this brings about a revision of what determines the human as human. It is beyond the scope of this work to elaborate how and where Heidegger undertook his project to "destabilize logic" which, like the "destructuring of the history of ontology," is a forerunner of "the overcoming of metaphysics."[157] In the context of the mid-1930s, it is undeniable that this project is related to Heidegger's steps toward *muthos*, i.e., toward a "history of being" as a "mythology of the event of appropriation." Thus when he remarks in a passage from the first *Black Notebook* that "only someone who is German can in an originarily new way poetize being and say being," that "he alone will conquer anew the essence of *theōria* and finally create *logic*," this reveals the extent to which Heidegger's project to "destabilize logic" went hand in hand with the "metapolitics 'of' the historical people."[158]

The "destructuring of the history of ontology," i.e., the "destabilization of logic," takes its final shape with the so-called "overcoming of metaphysics." In a text written between 1936 and 1946 that bears this title – which omits the definite article and performatively transforms the text itself into an "overcoming" – Heidegger's "being-historical" interpretation of "history" becomes immediately clear. As the "*animal ratio-nale*," the human is "now" the "laboring animal" who must "wander through the desert of earth's desolation." A "decline" has "taken place," the "consequences" of which are "the events of world history in this century." This "decline" stems from the "completion of metaphysics" in Nietzsche's thinking. The "completion" furnishes the "scaffolding for an order of the earth which will supposedly last for a long time."[159] A "consequence" of this "metaphysical" historical process is the proclamation of a "superhumanity," to which the notion of "subhumanity" belongs when understood metaphysically. Here, the human being has become "the most important raw material" for its own "production." In a manner that, from the perspective of today, is nothing less than prophetic, Heidegger predicts that "some days factories will be built for the artificial breeding of human material, based on present-day chemical research."[160] Without completely leaving the Nazi Party, Heidegger clearly takes his distance from the "machina-tion" of National Socialism. The "overcoming of metaphysics" now detaches itself from the "metapolitics 'of' the historical people."

For Heidegger, "metaphysics" is the name of an epoch of "being" in which the latter was understood by way of concepts from the philosophy of Plato and Aristotle. This epoch comes to an end in Hegel's and Nietzsche's thought. In a very basic way, we can say that "metaphysical" thinking is fundamentally indifferent to the "distinction between being and beings." At one point, Heidegger writes:

> The difference between beings and being is shunted into the harmlessness of a merely represented ("logical") distinction,

provided metaphysics comes to know at all of this distinction itself as such, which, strictly speaking, metaphysics does not and cannot do. For metaphysical thinking indeed abides only *in* this distinction but such that in a certain sense being itself is understood as a kind of being.[161]

If, from Plato onward, "metaphysics" takes its point of departure from the distinction between the sensuous and the supersensuous, i.e., between materialism and idealism, then it "abides *in* this distinction" between "being" and "beings" without being able to interpret this "difference" in an adequate manner. Instead of thinking the difference between "being itself" and "beings," "metaphysics" understands "being" as "beingness" and grasps "being" as "presence and constancy."[162] For "metaphysical thinking," to the extent that the characteristics of "beings" are generalized into "beingness," "beings" are the starting point for any understanding whatsoever. We do not gain knowledge of what "conceals" and "withdraws" itself; it remains, like the notion of "difference *as* difference," "unthought."

If it is true that "metaphysics" furnishes the "scaffolding for an order of the earth which will supposedly last for a long time," the term "overcoming metaphysics" becomes, then, problematic; Heidegger himself saw this. "Metaphysics" cannot be abolished "like an opinion," "one can by no means leave it behind as a doctrine no longer believed and represented."[163] While the concept of "overcoming" suggests that one could, as it were, cross over an imaginary limit between one "history" and another, Heidegger nevertheless stresses the "duration" of this process which itself can only be a constant preoccupation with "metaphysics." Thus the "overcoming of metaphysics" leads straight into the paradox of always having to thematize "metaphysics" and its "fundamental concepts" time and again. However, this does not happen in an arbitrary way but rather in accordance with the "historical necessity" – which is no longer simply philosophical – of going through "metaphysics" in order to arrive at "another question" or "another thinking." This is why Heidegger claims that the "overcoming [*Überwindung*] of metaphysics" is better understood as the "recovery" (*Verwindung*) of metaphysics.[164] This concept indicates that something can be made to disappear only after a lengthy preoccupation with it. The "recovery" of an injury or sickness thus consists in a longer process in which the injured patient worries about getting better. On the one hand, this process happens of its own accord, given that the injury has to heal itself; on the other hand, the injured patient also "needs" to participate in this process, given that he might not be cured without this participation. According to this analogy, the "recovery of metaphysics" is something like a continuous thematization of "metaphysical thinking" in and through which "metaphysics" eventually "vanishes."

Nevertheless, the "overcoming of metaphysics" remains an unstable notion. Can there be thinking beyond the fundamental determinations that make this thinking possible to begin with? What happens when thinking actually abandons the premises of "science" and of "scientificity"? When it invalidates the "axioms" of logic? Can thinking unfold in a radically poetic manner that has been hitherto unknown? Unlike Habermas, whose legacy thoroughly accepts the rational standard of "metaphysics," Heidegger never spoke of "post-metaphysical" thought. He preferred instead to characterize his ponderings as a "transitional thinking" that "prepares for the other questioning."[165] From this standpoint, the Heideggerian "thought" of "overcoming metaphysics" amounts to reflection on and at the limits of "metaphysics," a "thinking" that is never simply and completely outside these determinations.

Language as the "house of being"

It is not an exaggeration to say that Heidegger began his academic career as a "logician." Both his dissertation and qualifying dissertation (*Habilitationsschrift*) dealt with the question of logic. His teacher Rickert predicted that he would "achieve great success" in this field. During his lecture courses in the 1920s, Heidegger saw himself time and again confronted with the question of how we must adequately understand the original phenomenon of "logic," i.e., the *logos* itself. Heidegger initially turns to the texts of Plato and Aristotle; later, in the 1930s, Heraclitus' concept of *logos* comes to the fore.

In *Being and Time*, we find a condensed version of Heidegger's engagement with this question, which had by then already lasted a decade. *Logos* is here understood as an "existential," what Heidegger calls "discourse" (*Rede*). This translation is justified by the fact that Aristotle thinks the *logos* as a *deloun*, i.e., as that which makes manifest "what is being talked about" in discourse. This was Heidegger's point of departure for thinking through the phenomenon of "language" (*Sprache*). "Discourse" is the "existential-ontological foundation" of language.[166] "Language" is simply the "way in which discourse gets expressed."[167] In language, "significations" are brought to "words": "Words accrue to significations. But word-things are not provided with significations," writes Heidegger without explaining how it is possible for this difference between "word" and "signification" to emerge in the first place.[168]

"Discourse" is "the 'significant' structuring of the intelligibility of being-in-the-world," to which "being-with" belongs. Initially, "discourse" is thus everything that happens linguistically in the encounter with the other, an encounter that strives from the start toward clarification. "Listening and silence" are, in a particular manner, part and parcel of this encounter. The analysis of "silence," which played such a major role in Heidegger's thinking during the 1930s, is one of *Being and Time*'s phenomenological climaxes. Heidegger's analysis of "discourse" thus generates a host of results. It is not clear, however, how this analysis can possibly provide a "foundation" for a "completely sufficient definition of language."

Even though the analysis in *Being and Time* that grounds language in discourse does not yield satisfying results, we can nevertheless discern in this set-up an intention that will later attain its full philosophical significance. Heidegger explains that Greek logic furnishes the "foundation" of the "grammar" of Indo-European languages. This logic is in turn based on "an ontology of what is present."[169] We can see here the problem that repeatedly led Heidegger to investigate the "essence of language." As the "foundation" of "grammar," the "ontology of what is present" rests on the distinction of an underlying present-at-hand thing that can be predicated of different attributes. What Aristotle calls the *hupokeimenon* (literally, "what lies under"), to which the *sumbebēkota* (properties) are then attributed, shows up again in "grammar" as the distinction between subject and predicate. The verbal noun "being" is grammatically described as a copula, the "bond" which binds subject and predicate: S *is* P. For Heidegger, however, "being" is neither a "thing" which could be predicated of "properties" – it would be "a being" if it could – nor is it reducible to the function of the copula. But how can language take up "being" if the latter evades a fundamental aspect of language, namely, the subject–predicate relation of the copula? How can we speak of something that has no place in language's grammar?

After 1933, Heidegger deals with this problem in his "metapolitical" lecture courses. There he takes up a theme that had already preoccupied him in his dissertation. In the 1933–4 winter semester lecture course titled "On the Essence of Truth," Heidegger claims that "reflection on *logos* as the theory of *language*, that is *grammar*, is dominated at the same time by logic as the theory of thinking."[170] By "*destabilizing the grammatical representations of language*," we must bring an end to the dominion of "logic."[171] This can only happen if the "essence of language" is thematized.

At the end of the summer semester lecture course of 1934, this "destabilization" is achieved. Heidegger writes: "The essence of language essences where it happens as world-forming power, that is, where it in advance performs and brings into jointure the being of beings. The original language is the language of poetry."[172] Regardless of the "metapolitical" implications of this thought, the newly articulated "destabilization of logic" deals with the problem of how language could adequately express "being" if the latter evades language's "grammatical representations."[173] From this point on, "poetry" begins to play a key role in Heidegger's philosophy. The question is whether every single type of language is "objectifying," whether every thought has to be an "object." Does speaking necessarily mean to objectify?

In *Contributions to Philosophy*, Heidegger formulates this problem in a striking manner: "In ordinary language, which is ever more comprehensively used up today and degraded through idle chatter, the truth of beyng cannot be said. Can this truth be said immediately in the least, if all language is indeed the language of beings? Or can a new language be devised for beyng? No."[174] The "language of beings" is based on a "grammar" that goes back to an "ontology of what is present." This was precisely the problem Heidegger struggled with in *Contributions to Philosophy*. Boycotting public philosophical discourse was his temporary solution to this problem. He then publishes an esoteric text that abandons the norms of public discourse in order to address a particular audience, i.e., "the few."[175] Yet, as late as 1962, Heidegger concludes one of his last lectures with the suggestion that "the saying of the event of appropriation in the form of a lecture remains itself an obstacle" because a lecture "speaks merely in propositional sentences."[176] At the beginning of the lecture, he stresses that "the point is not to listen to a series of propositions, but rather to follow the movement of showing," a remark that recalls Wittgenstein's *Tractatus Logico-Philosophicus*.[177]

In *Contributions to Philosophy*, Heidegger develops his question concerning a "new language for beyng" by means of the following thoughts: a "language of beyng" must be "one that speaks."[178] He adds: "All saying must allow the co-emergence of a capacity to hear it. Both saying and hearing must be of the same origin." This "transformation of language" leads to a "transformed saying." The "origin" of "saying" and the "capacity to hear" is, of course, "beyng." Heidegger calls attention to the "responsive" character of a relation according to which the "saying" relates and answers to something from which it itself originates. Thus the "language of beyng" is not a language *about* "beyng"; rather, the "language of beyng" is "beyng" itself as "language." In this sense, the "saying" must already be in itself a "capacity to hear" "beyng" itself. "Hearing" marks the distinction that exists between "saying" and "beyng."

Heidegger develops this thought further in *On the Way to Language*, a 1954 volume that gathers important lectures and other texts. This work contains the following sentences which are often cited and criticized: "Language speaks. The human being speaks [*spricht*] insofar as he corresponds [*entspricht*] to language. To correspond is to hear."[179] The notion that "language speaks" is a radicalization of an experience that is self-evident. Language is an active system of meanings that makes it possible for a human being – who each time grows up in a given linguistic environment – to express himself in this way or that without having single-handedly "made" that language himself.[180] When we refer to the French language, we of course do not imply that contemporary French speakers have "produced" French or that someone who wants to speak French would have to "fabricate" it first. Rather, this person must learn an already existing language by hearing it. It is in this sense that a language precedes its respective speakers.

On the other hand, there is no language without its speakers. Thus, Heidegger emphasizes, "We do not fully think through the sentence 'Language speaks' as long as we ignore the following issue: In order to speak in its own way, language needs, that is to say, requires human speaking which, as a way of corresponding, is in turn needed, i.e., useful for language [...]."[181] As in the aforementioned "responsive" structure of the "event of appropriation" and the relation between "saying" and "hearing," Heidegger's point of departure for understanding the relation between "language" and "speaking" is a reciprocal "need." Speaking is no longer a mere human faculty but an "act of correspondence." The fact that the human being is the living being who speaks means that this property that distinguishes the human from all other (known) forms of beings is not something the human simply gives himself; rather, the human being receives it from language.

That being said, it is still not clear how such a conception of language "corresponds" to "being itself" as opposed to another conception of language that is grounded in "logic." According to Heidegger, "to correspond" is "to hear." Now, this "hearing" is able to relate to something that is always already given in advance: words, sentences, texts, etc. Admittedly, if a thinking of "being itself" has not developed beyond this point, it will face the problem of "objectification" which consists in the fact that the word "being" remains subjugated to an "ontology of what is present." This is the reason why, in corresponding, "hearing" does not relate to words or sentences, precisely, but to something that precedes them. Heidegger calls it the "peal of stillness."[182] Words and sentences seem to spring from a source that does not yet appear in the form of words and sentences. The absence of words and sentences is characterized as "stillness." Due to the fact that the latter gathers *all* words and sentences – and "hearing" as well – unto itself, Heidegger speaks of its "peal" (*Geläut*).[183] However, isn't it the case that the expression "peal of stillness" also remains an acoustic metaphor? Which does not really solve the problem of how it is possible for "being itself" to evade the propositional statement.

Be that as it may, Heidegger has another reason for dispelling the logical conception of language. In "formal logic," language is taken to be a structure that is indifferent to its content matter. The sentence model "S is P" tells us nothing about what "S" and "P" are. It is supposed to provide merely a pattern that can linguistically express everything that exists. If we transpose this formal structure onto the everyday notion of means and ends, it then seems plausible to argue that language's function is to communicate the content matter to us. In this sense, we conceive of language as an "instrument" or "medium" in and through which "information" is generated. Heidegger fundamentally rejects this mathematical and cybernetic conception of language espoused by Norbert Wiener at the end of the 1940s.[184] This view technologically eliminates essential aspects of language – aspects which poetry exhibits. In poetry, a certain kind of "speaking" becomes manifest that is not reducible to pieces of information. This is the understanding of language Heidegger is opposing when he writes the following famous sentences:

> Thinking accomplishes the relation of being to the essence of the human being. It does not make or cause the relation. Thinking brings this relation to being solely as something handed over to thought itself from being. Such offering consists in the fact that in thinking being comes to language. Language is the house of being. In its home human beings dwell.[185]

Language is much more than a simple "medium" or "instrument" at the disposal of human beings who can then control things and themselves as they become "informed." Even though language can appear as "information," it also harbors possibilities that go far beyond that. This beyond is what is at stake. Heidegger's philosophy grasps language as a "dwelling" in which the human being "dwells." In an emphatic sense, this "dwelling" can exist only if "being comes to language." From this point of view, we see how different the conception of language as "information" is from the view of language as "house of being"; this difference is decisive for "dwelling." For Heidegger, a world dominated by the cybernetic conception of language has eliminated the possibility of "dwelling."

God and "the gods"

"Only a God can save us."[186]

At its beginning, Heidegger's intellectual biography is profoundly linked to the Catholicism that was so alive in the southwestern provinces of Germany. In a text from the late 1930s titled "My Pathway Hitherto," Heidegger expressed this as follows:

> And who would not want to recognize that a confrontation with Christianity reticently accompanied my entire path hitherto, a confrontation that was not, and is not, a "problem" that one "takes up" to address but a preservation of, and at the same time a painful separation from, one's ownmost provenance: the parental home, homeland and youth. Only the one who was so rooted in an actually lived Catholic world may be able to have an inkling of the necessities that like subterranean quakes have been at work in the pathway of my inquiry hitherto.[187]

There is a kernel of truth to this dramatization of the "pathway hitherto." Heidegger's thinking is marked by a "a confrontation [*Auseinandersetzung*] with Christianity" even in places where it is not all apparent on the surface of the text. The "history of being" is a narrative in which the "historical" significance of Christianity plays a key role, precisely. This importance eventually reappears in Heidegger's anti-Semitic statements from the beginning of the 1940s. During this period, the "confrontation with Christianity" seems to have been carried out in a literal sense: Heidegger's thought and Christianity were "positioned against each other" (*auseinander gesetzt*).

Yet the "path" leading up to this parting was long. The important Marburg lecture "Phenomenology and Theology" from 1928 was one step in this direction. To put it crudely, what is at stake in this lecture is the distinction between Christian theology and a philosophy that understands itself as ontology. Heidegger describes the former as a "positive science."[188] Here "positive" simply means that theology investigates the more or less clearly demarcated object of "Christianity." One does not need any "philosophy" in order to be a devout "Christian" or a believer. "The positive science of faith" needs philosophy only in regard to its "scientific character." Apart from this superficial dependency – as Heidegger saw it – there is such a rift between "faith" and "philosophy" that, over and against the "*specific possibility of existence* that essentially belongs to *philosophy*," Heidegger characterizes "faith" as philosophy's "mortal enemy." Let us note in passing that Heidegger by no means speaks of "theology" itself in this passage but of the "facticity of faith." "Faith" and "philosophy" constitute such a radical opposition that "philosophy does not even begin to want in any way to do battle with it." Given that "philosophy" is essentially different from the "specific possibility of existence" of "faith," it leaves the latter, as it were, intact.

Five years later, in the famous Rectorial Address, "The Self-Assertion of the German University," Heidegger refers to the possibility that "our ownmost existence [Dasein] itself stands on the threshold a great transformation." For "it may be true what the last German philosopher to passionately seek God, Friedrich Nietzsche, said: 'God is dead.'"[189] This remark is anything but empty rhetoric. Heidegger's project to have "another inception" (with "the Germans") respond to a "first inception" (with "the Greeks") does not simply give rise to a difference between Christianity and philosophy that would make it impossible for these two to coexist, as it were. Like Nietzsche, Heidegger here blames Christianity itself for the foreclosure of certain philosophical possibilities that emerged in the context of the "first inception."

It is undeniably the case that Heidegger took very seriously Nietzsche's famous aphorism (125), "the madman," from a text titled *The Gay Science*.[190] For Heidegger, the death of the Christian God and His transformation into a moribund "Christian culture" were a "historical" fact. This also explains Heidegger's numerous attacks against Christianity in the *Black Notebooks*.[191] This religion was now useless vis-à-vis the "other inception"; on the contrary, as Heidegger held the idea of a "creator God" to be complicit with "machination," this notion was anything but "inceptive."

It is important to see how Heidegger interprets this bitter insight of Nietzsche's "madman." Without a doubt, Nietzsche is thinking of the Christian God here. "We" have "killed" this God because we no longer see in the Gospels a binding order for "our" lives. Yet something else is at stake with the Christian God. In this Nietzschean aphorism, Heidegger takes "God" to be the "name for the realm of ideas and the ideal," that is to say, the name for the sphere of the "supersensuous" pure and simple, which has persisted in European philosophy from Plato onward.[192] With the death of the Christian God and the vanishing of this "supersensuous" sphere, all the moral and ethical criteria that once organized our lives lose their credibility. The absolute standard around which all other standards revolved has disappeared: "Is there still an up and down? Aren't we straying as though through an infinite nothing?", asks the "madman." With the death of God, the "being-historical" epoch of "nihilism" irrupts.

However, Nietzsche is not the only one to notice the death of God in the European world. Hölderlin, too, spoke of the "flight of the gods"; the poet counted Jesus Christ as one god among these.[193] Like Nietzsche, Hölderlin did not lose sight of the possibility of the return of the divine. It is often said that this discourse on the collapse of the Christian notion of God, together with the return of other "gods" – a discourse initiated not only by Hölderlin or Nietzsche but also by Schelling and, in the twentieth century, Stefan George, Rilke, and even Ernst Jünger – emerged as a particularly German discourse that left noticeable traces in Heidegger's thought. There was no similar phenomenon in France.

On the one hand, the message of the "madman" is an undeniable fact for Heidegger. Over the course of two thousand years of European history, the power of the Christian God has become weak. On the other hand, he does not let go of the notion that the divine can appear "once again" in the world after the disappearance of God. Had he not already talked about the philosophers who "seek the God" in the Rectorial Address? Here the definite article indicates that Heidegger was not thinking of the Christian God, who can never be addressed in such a manner. Accordingly, Heidegger also agreed with Hölderlin's groundbreaking description of a godforsaken epoch of "being" as a "night" into which the "gods" have withdrawn themselves in order to wait for a "morning" to come.[194]

In the immediate context of the Rectorial Address, however, Heidegger initially attempted to use Hölderlin's poetry of the "gods" for "metapolitical" purposes. No doubt thinking of what he had developed in the Rectorial Address, Heidegger takes up the following lines from Hölderlin: "but when / a God appears upon Heaven and earth and sea / Comes all-renewing clarity" in such a way that he makes the "people" dependent upon an "originally unitary experience of being bound in return to the Gods."[195] In this sense, at issue is "the true appearing or non-appearing of the God in the being of the people from out of the need of its beyng, and for such beyng."[196] Hölderlin was supposed to have been the "founder of German beyng" insofar as he gave the "people" a new "bond," i.e., a new *re-ligio*.[197] To be sure, this fundamentally blasphemous thought disappears as soon as Heidegger abandons the project of a "metapolitics 'of' the historical people." Nevertheless, this thought again played a major role in the narrative of the "mytho-logy of the event of appropriation."

The reference to the "gods" merits an explanation. In his poems, Hölderlin draws on divine figures familiar to us from the ancient myths of European history. His poems praise, above all, the Greek gods and demi-gods such as Apollo, Dionysus, Heracles – as well as Jesus Christ. For Hölderlin, the gods are not dead cultural objects but the presently living forms of a myth. However, these familiar European names are not the only ones we find in Hölderlin's poetry. Thus very often Hölderlin speaks simply of a "father" or of a mysterious figure, i.e., the "god of gods" or the "prince of the feast." We cannot classify these figures in accordance with the familiar names from our canon of gods.

Initially, Heidegger does not take up Hölderlin's description of these "gods." In *Contributions to Philosophy*, Heidegger speaks of the problem of polytheism. The use of the plural "gods" is not supposed to "affirm the existence of many gods instead of one." Rather, this is supposed to express an "unde-cidability."[198] It is meant to be left "undecided" whether or not the "gods" or "a God" can be present "once more." Heidegger leaves open exactly what these "gods" or the "god" will look like. Nevertheless, this "undecidability" is not supposed to be an "empty possibility"; from out of this "undecidability," a "decision" should be made, namely, the decision of whether a divine epiphany may or may not still happen.

It is worth mentioning that Heidegger does not stop at this "undecidability." Taking one step closer, as it were, to a "decision," Heidegger capitalizes on his narrative of the "history of being." Hölderlin announces the appearance of a "God still to come" ("Bread and Wine," tenth stanza); Heidegger's thinking takes this up in turn. At the end of the introduction to *Mindfulness* – a text that, as the unfolding of the "history of being," is in close proximity to *Contributions to Philosophy* – Heidegger indicates that "the unique service of the not yet appeared but announced god" belongs to the happening of the "truth of beyng" and the "clearing of self-concealment" which has "grounded" the human being as Dasein. As Heidegger says in *Contributions to Philosophy*, this "god" is the "last god." Hölderlin's poetry "announced" him, which of course does not mean that Heidegger cannot speak about this god in a way entirely different from the poet – something he in fact does.

It is particularly difficult to determine the narrative figure of the "last god." Heidegger speaks about this last god without clearly inserting him into a theological context known to us. This has led several commentators to relate certain passages – such as, for example, the "passing by of the last god" – back to biblical formulations (Exodus 2: 22), a tried and tested hermeneutical practice that nevertheless misses the point here.[199] For Heidegger speaks of the "last god" as "wholly other than past ones and especially other than the Christian one."[200] The characterization of "lastness" seems to give us a clue of sorts. In the "being-historical" epoch of the "abandonment by beyng," only a "god" can be the point of departure for "opening up an entirely different time-space."[201] The association between "lastness" and "disclosure," or the notion of transforming the end of time into an arrival or Parousia, corresponds to the familiar notion of "eschatology" in Christian theology. As a temporal and spatial determination, the *eschathon* is what is outermost or last. At the end of times, God reveals Himself one more time in order to judge humanity. Over and against this, Heidegger speaks of an "eschatology of being."[202] As "historical," "being" is "itself eschatological." The Christian idea of a final revelation at the end of times is thus derivative with respect to an "eschatology of being."

The so-called *Spiegel* interview with Rudolf Augstein – who traveled to Todtnauberg to interview Heidegger in 1966 – attests to how the narratival figure of the "last god" is part and parcel of an eschatological narrative. Here Heidegger writes the famous words: "Philosophy will not be able to effect an immediate transformation of the present condition of the world. This is not only true of philosophy, but of all merely human thought and endeavor. Only a god can save us."[203] Heidegger repeatedly makes use of an article when talking about this "god." It would no doubt be overly facile to argue that Heidegger is thinking here of the "last god." However, the situation is similar to that of *Contributions to Philosophy*. The "forgetting of being" dominates the "present condition of the world." It is no longer a "transformation" that is at stake but a "saving." In an increasingly dramatic manner, Heidegger once again touches on the revolutionary kernel of his thinking, this time investing it with the theological narrative of "salvation."

Whereas Heidegger's philosophical beginning is tied to that Catholic "magic" of the "scent of fir and candles," his later thinking is interested in a different kind of "magic." At one point, Heidegger himself evokes his "anti-Christianity."[204] He was not a "Christian" because, "Christianly speaking, he did not have grace." Heidegger's decision in favor of philosophy was, no doubt, a decision against theology and its Christianity, which in other places is explicitly distinguished from "Christendom."[205] "Faith" remained a radical and impugnable alternative to thought; it remained thought's "mortal enemy." Nevertheless, the words of the "madman" are applicable to a "Christendom" that has become ordinary.

And yet Heidegger's "anti-Christianity" is by no means to be understood (simply) as a sober and reserved attitude toward "faith" and "grace." In *Observations IV* – one of the *Black Notebooks* from the 1940s – Heidegger remarks at one point that "Jehovah" is "the god" who "presumed to be the elected God and tolerated no other gods beside Him."[206] He then asks: "What is a god who ascends to the elected god over and against the other gods? At any rate, he is 'never' the absolute god, assuming that this could even be divine."

Whereas in *Contributions to Philosophy* Heidegger wishes to suspend the difference between monotheism and polytheism in an "undecidability," he is more emphatic here. The "modern systems of total tyranny" originate in "Judeo-Christian monotheism."[207] Heidegger again adopts the same anti-Semitic strategy: if he does not exactly invert the relationship between perpetrator and victim, i.e., between Germans and Jews, he certainly levels it down to an equivalence or neutralization. The "Judeo-Christian monotheism" and "Jehovah," who has made Himself into the "elected God," betray a multiplicity of gods and prepare the way for the "modern systems of total tyranny." By contrast, the anti-Roman, anti-confessional, anti-universal, and, of course, anti-Semitic movement of National Socialism had great sympathy for poets, thinkers, and composers who privileged the "gods" over the one and only "God" of monotheism. During the period of National Socialism, Heidegger's "anti-Christianity" was in no way an unusual phenomenon.

4

The "Essence of Technology"

Friedrich Nietzsche and Ernst Jünger

Heidegger had already spent nearly twenty years dealing with the "essence of technology" by the early 1950s when, as Rüdiger Safranski writes, "Heidegger's term *Gestell* [positionality], as a designation for the technological world, was making the rounds in Germany."[1] Gradually, technology became one of Heidegger's major themes.

In a 1935 text titled "The Rectorate 1933/34," Heidegger remarks that, in 1932, he had already studied and "thoroughly discussed" Ernst Jünger's essay "Total Mobilization" and his book *The Worker*; in addition, he had also read the 1934 essay "On Pain" very closely.[2] Heidegger argues that these texts express an "essential understanding of Nietzsche's metaphysics" "insofar as the history and present of the western world are seen and foreseen within the horizon of this metaphysics." Jünger and Nietzsche are the two figures who initially inspired Heidegger's interpretation of technology, first as "machination" and subsequently as "positionality." It was presumably thanks to the aforementioned texts by Jünger that Heidegger initially grasped technology as a philosophical problem.

This does not mean that Heidegger had not earlier dealt with problems that derive from the "technological world." In *Being and Time*, the analysis of "the they" is related to this phenomenon. The philosopher reminds us of the leveling effect of "utilizing public transportation" or the "use of information services such as the newspaper"; yet it was Jünger who first gestured toward the epochal novelty of modern technology.[3]

Jünger's essays attempt to understand how a new "type" of human being makes its historical appearance following the "battles of material" of World War I. A "type" is a kind of model or standard. Technology determines the "type" in advance. Drawing on a military lexicon, Jünger characterizes technology as a "total mobilization," i.e., a setting in motion of every area of our lives and of the world.

In the "battles of material" of World War I, Jünger sees in the "soldier" the "type" of man capable of measuring up to this "total mobilization." In his war diaries, such as the "Storm of Steel" (1920) or "Copse 125" (1925), Jünger had described the everyday life of war. The "soldier" knows that as an individual he is not what matters in this daily routine; he has to carry out his "work" as perfectly as possible. The "machine" fits in to this as the "expression of the human will to master matter."[4] The soldier must "fuse" with the "machine"; a "technological instinct" must "run in his blood."

For Jünger, the soldier's worldview became the "typical" way of life after World War I. The "type" of this way of life is now no longer the "soldier" but the "worker." He no longer thinks of his life as the possibility of personal happiness but as a task: to serve the will to power and, in so doing, to gain power himself. We must organize the world in accordance with "total mobilization." The worker's "type" is by no means an economic or sociological phenomenon but a "metaphysical" figure. Heidegger argues that, to the extent that Jünger still uses the concepts of "type" or "figure," he remains stuck in the tradition of Platonic thought. Therefore, the "overcoming" of metaphysics has to be concerned with Jünger's texts as well.

In *The Worker*, Jünger arrives at the following definition of technology: "technology is the way in which the form of the worker mobilizes the world."[5] The phenomenon that Jünger has in mind lies close at hand. It is a matter of an omnipresent acceleration of human beings, machines, and information. In his essay, Jünger goes through every sector systematically – he interprets sports and leisure activities in general as work

– so as to observe everywhere the increase of business, speed, and energy consumption.

Heidegger rightly calls attention to the fact that Jünger's way of thinking results from his being a disciple and inheritor of Nietzsche. For Jünger, Nietzsche is the philosopher of the "will to power" and of the "overman." The essay on the "worker" is influenced by some of Nietzsche's main ideas, for example his late and exoteric notions that "life" is a "will to power" or that an unconditional "affirmation" takes the human beyond himself and leads him to the "overman." In a fragment from his notebooks – which Jünger knew from the edition of *Will to Power* available at the time – Nietzsche establishes a link between "soldier" and "worker": "Workers should learn to feel like soldiers." The point is "to position the individual so that he can achieve the *highest possible accomplishment each time according to his kind.*"[6] During his earlier phase of an apotheosis of the machine, Nietzsche is thinking along similar lines:

> *The machine as teacher.* The machine of itself teaches the mutual cooperation of hordes of men in operations where each man has to do only one thing: it provides the model for the party apparatus and the conduct of warfare. On the other hand, it does not teach individual autocracy: it makes of many *one* machine and of every individual an instrument to *one* end. Its most generalized effect is to teach the utility of centralization.[7]

Taking these proto-cybernetic ideas as his point of departure, Jünger was able to develop his metaphysics of "total mobilization" and "of the worker" in a highly original and suggestive manner.

There was, however, another reason why Heidegger thought that he could build on Jünger's discourse of "total mobilization." In his essay on "Total Mobilization," Jünger initially describes it as a "mode of organizational thinking," immediately adding that "Total Mobilization is merely an intimation of that higher mobilization that the age is discharging upon us."[8] The reference to our "time" and to a collective subject was bound to attract Heidegger's attention. The allusion to Nietzsche at the conclusion of Jünger's essay confirmed Heidegger's impression: "And for this reason, the new form of armament, in which we have already for some time been implicated, must be a mobilization of the German – nothing else."[9] Two years later in *The Worker*, Jünger was even clearer about this: "And here is what we believe: that the dawn of the worker means the same thing as a new beginning for Germany." Heidegger could reasonably believe that he had found a "metapolitical" ally in Jünger.

In the Matriculation Address of November 1933, Heidegger emphatically refers to Jünger's *The Worker*: "On the basis of the experience of the world war's battles of material, Jünger designated purely and simply the mode of being to come of the human of the next epoch *through the figure* of the worker."[10] In this way, Jünger provides a paradigm for the "students" of the future: "This new type of student no longer 'studies,' that is to say, no longer sits sheltered somewhere simply 'aspiring' to something while remaining seated. This new type of those who desire to know is continually on the way. And those students will become *workers*."[11] Heidegger seems to have engaged with Jünger's figure of the "worker" against the backdrop of his "metapolitical" reflections. "Work" transposes and configures "the people within the field affected by all the essential powers of being [...]. The National-Socialist State is a work State."[12] In the wake of the "metapolitics 'of' the historical people," was Heidegger prepared to accept technology as "total mobilization"?

Three or four years later, in one of the *Black Notebooks*, Heidegger again draws on Jünger's concept of "total mobilization." Technology is "neither grasped 'metaphysically' – in the truth and untruth of beyng – nor mastered at all, by postulating it to be the 'total' determination of Dasein."[13] It lies "in the essence" of technology that it should "become this." Yet how is this "to be endured"? "Through mere recognition," as Jünger suggests it? Heidegger rejects this possibility and adds that we must "come to terms with the possibility that through the 'total mobilization' of the technological itself everything is pressed to its end, especially if the sources of a possible surpassing of this occurrence are nowhere opened up." This becomes possible only when "we go back very far in *historical* meditation – to the connection between *tēchnē, alētheia*, and *ousia*." To sum up: "Only on the basis of a questioning of beyng and of its truth does the *space* of a confrontation with technology arise for us [...]."

This was Heidegger's plan for approaching "technology" in a philosophical manner.

By the time Heidegger publicly interprets Jünger's *The Worker* one more time in a polemical way, in the context of a "small circle of colleagues" in the early 1940s, Jünger had become for him a "metaphysical bourgeois."[14] Now, next to Oswald Spengler, Heidegger considers Jünger a "contemporaneous literati," i.e., "one of the best translate."[15,16] In 1939, Jünger published a novella titled *On the Marble Cliffs*, which could very well be understood as a sinister parable of National Socialism. For Heidegger, this novella was merely an expression of the "disarray at the heart of the completed epoch of metaphysics (Nietzsche)."[17] Yet Heidegger saw in the concept of "total mobilization" a kind of challenge that ultimately led him to come up with, as Safranski suggests, the legendary "term 'positionality' as a designation for the technological world."

"Machination" and "positionality"

Heidegger's philosophy of technology originates in the "questioning concerning beyng and the truth of beyng," that is to say, it has a place in the narrative of the "history of being." This means that Heidegger does not consider technology as an isolated phenomenon; rather, he always links it to a history that has lasted 2,500 years. Therefore, to understand technology – or the technological – means to interpret and explain this history. This in turn leads Heidegger to associate the history of technology with the emergence of the word *technē*. As always, the "history of being" begins with "the Greeks."

Heidegger's engagement with technology and the "Greeks" consists almost exclusively in his translation and interpretation of the first choral ode of Sophocles' *Antigone*. In Heidegger's translation, this begins with the following words:

Manifold is the uncanny, yet nothing
Uncannier than man bestirs itself, rising up beyond him.[18]

Sophocles relates the characterization of the human being as the absolute "uncanniest" to the human ability to exploit nature. Sophocles uses the word *technē* and links it to another verb, *to machanoen*. The word is related to the adjective *"mechanikos,"* meaning "ingenious," "skillful," "clever." Heidegger translates *to machanoen* (human aptitude) as an "ingenuity" that is supposed to be clever (*sophon*).[19] Whom does this ingenuity characterize? Technology (*technē*). Sophocles emphasizes the ambivalent and indeed tragic nature of technology in a different way than the other philosophers who speak of *technē* – such as, for example, Aristotle who was born roughly twenty years after Sophocles' death and who dealt with this concept in the *Nicomachean Ethics* (1140 a10). The greatness of human beings is indeed apparent in the clever ingenuity and craftsmanship of the species. However, these seduce the human to be bold and daring (*tolma*), thereby always running the risk of failing.

At the beginning of the modern period, René Descartes takes a decisive step in the "history of being" toward the importance of technology. According to Heidegger, Descartes turns "beings" into measurable and calculable objects on the basis of which the human being starts to understand himself as a subject. The "objectification of beings" is accomplished in "a setting before, a re-presenting [*Vor-stellen*], aimed at bringing each being before it in such a way that the man who calculates can be sure – and that means certain – of the being."[20] Descartes indeed determines truth as certainty (*certitudo*), that is to say, as a truth that can be tested by a subject who then establishes it once and for all. Related to this is the fact that Descartes could make use of the technological inventions of the early modern period, such as the microscope or telescope. This fits well with Descartes's description of the human being as *"maître et possesseur de la nature"* (master and possessor of nature) in the *Discours de la méthode* from 1637. Technology becomes "machination."

The use of the concept of "machination" is not unproblematic. Heidegger himself indicates that "conventionally, the term 'machination' refers to human undertakings that are intent on gaining advantages and on deception under the semblance of harmless activities."[21] *This* notion of "machination" does not go far enough in grasping the form of technology within the "history of being" that corresponds to Jünger's notion of "total mobilization." "Machination" names "that essence of being that decisively places all beings into makeability and malleability."[22] All "beings" are "always already" considered from the perspective of making and producing. If, as became apparent in the modern period, "machination" is the "essence of being," then the priority of "machination" as a "human undertaking" is no longer possible. Nevertheless, Heidegger is also thinking here along the lines of a reciprocal relationship of "need." As a "human comportment," "machination first comes into play to an unrestrained degree where the human kind in question already stands in the midst of beings whose being, as power, intensifies its essence to the extreme of machination."[23] In this sense, "human" "machination" can only happen if it is preceded by a "being-historical machination." Regardless of who the agent of "machination" may be at a given point – National Socialism, Bolshevism, Americanism, or "World-Judaism" – the latter can never function as the origin of "machination." This, of course, in no way changes the fact that, for Heidegger, there is a certain "humanity" that is particularly well suited to face the challenge of "machination."

We can already see the problems with Heidegger's conceptual choice. In the mid-1930s, as Heidegger characterizes the "essence of technology" as "machination," he inevitably ascribes a moral value to this "essence." The *Black Notebooks* corroborate this impression, especially as Heidegger reflects on *"technology and uprootedness."* "Radio and every sort of organization" have destroyed "the inner growth, i.e., the constant regrowth, into the tradition of the village and thereby destroy[ed] the village itself."[24] "Professorships for the 'sociology' of peasantry are instituted and heaps of books are written about nationality." However, all of this is part and parcel of "uprootedness," a phenomenon we must understand as a consequence of "machination."

On the basis of this phenomenon of "uprootedness," Heidegger speaks of the "corrupted history of machination."[25] Therefore, Heidegger initially ascribes an extremely pernicious role to the "essence of technology" within the "history of being." "Machination" destroys "history" and makes it impossible. Heidegger is thus trying to counteract a certain tension at the heart of "being itself." It is a matter of "disrupting history through the leap into the overcoming of metaphysics, and thereby to help to raise beings as a whole out of the hinges of machination."[26] This is the "freeing into freedom for the truth of being." To put it differently, Heidegger claims that "machination" exhibits an "essence" that we must "over-come." His hypothesis is that we must "free" ourselves from this "essence of technology."

It is entirely under the banner of this "freeing" that Heidegger reflects on the destructive events of World War II. At one point, Heidegger remarks that "*this* 'machination,'" i.e., "machination" in the sense of "human undertaking," is at most a distant consequence of being-historical machination; however, it is precisely this human "machination" that is Heidegger's main focus.[27] It thus becomes clear that, in the final analysis, "over-coming" "machination" is possible only if "machination" is driven to "self-annihilation."[28] Heidegger's affirmation of the destructive events of World War II follows this logic: the more ingrained the traces this destruction leaves behind, the more likely it is for "metaphysics," i.e., "machination," to be "over-come."

Apart from the fact that this notion is problematic from a moral standpoint – a problem that worsens as Heidegger grants the "Germans" a "sacrificial" role in the war vis-à-vis the "truth of being" and identifies the "essence of technology" with "what is essentially 'Jewish'" – we cannot understand the "essence of technology" in this way.[29] As we grasp this "essence" as "machination," we interpret it from the start as an evil "power" that must ultimately annihilate itself in order to make room for another "essence of being," i.e., the "freedom for the truth of beyng." This idea remains stuck in a *Manichean narrative* in which technology is always bound to appear as an evil. However, were technology to belong to "being," it would no longer be possible to denounce it as "machination," in spite of all the factually negative phenomena such as war and genocide.

The collapse of the Third Reich in May 1945 coincides with a break in Heidegger's thought. It is not simply with respect to the problem of technology that the philosopher has to orient himself anew. The narrative of the "history of being" had to be rewritten. The role of the "Germans" as guardians of the "other inception" came to an end. Heidegger knew that he could no longer be a public advocate for this Hölderlinian idea. Another situation came to pass in the "history of being."

"Machination" had not annihilated itself. The dramatic aspect of the narrative of a "decline" then gave way to a disillusionment that produced a change in the tone of Heidegger's thought.[30] The "technological world" persisted through every single destructive occurrence. Given these transformed conditions, technology had to be considered anew.

In December 1949, when Heidegger delivered a cycle of lectures entitled "Insight into That Which Is" to the prestigious Bremen Club, his audience witnessed a transformation in the technique of his thought. The concept of "machination" disappears. The semantic field of "positioning" (*Stellen*) replaces that of "making." "Beings" become "standing reserve through requisitioning."[31] "What does 'to position, place, set' [*stellen*] mean?" asks Heidegger, initially referring to the phrases: "to represent something [*etwas vor-stellen*], to produce something [*etwas her-stellen*]." Yet for Heidegger, *stellen* also means "to challenge forth, to demand, to compel towards self-positioning," in short "conscription [*Gestellung*]."[32] On the other hand, *stellen* happens with respect to nature. Technology positions nature, challenges it forth so it can "exploit" its raw materials. Thus what "essences" in nature becomes "standing reserve"; yet the human being, too, is "positioned" (*gestellt*). Technology positions the human and challenges forth nature. At the same time, technology positions itself and makes itself into "standing reserve." "Positioning" becomes total and sweeps everything up in its dynamic.

Thus Heidegger believes he can say the following: "Agriculture is now a mechanized food industry, in essence the same as the production of corpses in the gas chambers and extermination camps, the same as the blockading and starving of countries, the same as the production of hydrogen bombs."[33] The strategy of this remark is apparent. Heidegger wishes to show the extent to which even the human being has become "standing reserve." There is no "industrial" conception of "beings" against which the human could be protected. The human appears to have himself been made into a "raw material." Is the "production of corpses in the gas chambers and the extermination camps" not proof enough that this line has been crossed? What is problematic about this notion is not the particular formulation that Heidegger uses; we can find that in the work of Hannah Arendt as well.[34]

This statement reveals two problems. For Heidegger, the "essence" of the aforementioned phenomena is what is at stake. This essence would be "the same" everywhere. At the same time, Heidegger knew that it was not possible for his audience to agree with this thought from a moral point of view, a perspective he completely suppresses. Yet why would Heidegger want to claim that the "food industry" and the "production of corpses" are "in essence the same"? Is it not the case that Heidegger's sentence "works" only because he mentions in passing what is most horrifying, *as if* the latter went without saying? What does not get said here is that, from a moral point of view, food supply and mass murder are not at all in essence the same. It may very well be that this silence makes the rhetorical effect all the more powerful. Yet how can we justify using the Shoah for rhetorical effects?

About eight years earlier, in one of the *Black Notebooks*, Heidegger had expressed a similar thought but with a completely different formulation. There Heidegger referred to what is "essentially 'Jewish' in a metaphysical sense," which battles "against what is Jewish."[35] When this happens, "self-extermination" reaches a "climax in the history of being." This notion, too, draws on the knowledge that the "essence" is the "same" everywhere, that is to say, that the "Jewish essence," so to speak, is "the same" everywhere. Here this can only be synonymous with "machination." In this sense, there is a maximum of "self-extermination" when "what is Jewish battles against what is Jewish." Does this "self-extermination" not become manifest in the "production of corpses in the gas chambers and extermination camps"? In the Bremen Lectures, Heidegger alters, for obvious reasons, the formulation of an almost identical thought. He could not or did not want to name the unspeakable and heinous crimes of the Shoah.

Due to the dramatic nature of the lecture, the audience did not know at this point how this passage related to the text as a whole. Heidegger gestured toward other forms of *stellen*. "Requisitioning," he explains, comes upon "nature and history, humans and divinities"; it affects "all that is with conscription in view of its presence."[36] "Positionality" (*Ge-stell*) is "the self-gathered collection of positioning, wherein everything orderable essences."[37] Positionality "names the universal ordering, gathered of itself, of the complete orderability of what presences as a whole"; this is the Heideggerian inter-pretation of Jünger's total mobilization.

The formulation "what is in essence the same" thus acquires its authentic sense: "positionality" is the "essence" which makes everything the "same." "Positionality" – "essence of technology."[38] Heidegger emphasizes that "the essence of technology is nothing technological."[39] "Positionality" is nothing in the order of "beings." As Heidegger often remarks, not only is "positionality" nothing like "a being," it is rather the "first appearing of the event of appropriation."[40]

This notion, however, remains obscure. When Heidegger indicates that the essence of technology must "be thought for its part in its essence that is linked to the event," that it must be "at bottom understood first at the same time as the event," the long-standing "eschatological" character of Heidegger's philosophizing suddenly comes to the fore. We reach "the domain at the heart of which the hidden relation of the human being *in* the event to the event maintains the recovery of technology."[41] The "history of being" was not yet at an end. Its narrator could not let go of the idea of the "recovery of technology."

On the basis of his reading of Jünger's texts on "total mobilization," Heidegger decided that a philosophy of tech-nology would have to originate "in the question of beyng and its truth." The notion of "po-sitionality" corresponds to Hei-degger's last efforts as a philosopher of technology. Neverthe-less, this picture remains incomplete as long as we do not give an account of a different avenue that Heidegger's late thinking pursued.

Arrival in the "fourfold"?

Besides being the first place where the notion of "positional-ity" appears, the Bremen Lectures is also the text where the "fourfold" shows up for the first time.[42] "Po-sitionality" (*Ge-Stell*) and "fourfold" (*Geviert*) relate to each other in a specific way. In this connection, it is important to observe how Hei-degger introduces the thought of the "fourfold." Moreover, we must consider how this notion of "fourfold" is the last stage of Heidegger's "path of thought" that develops the problem of world.

In the context of the question of technology, Heidegger differentiates between "thing," "object," and "standing reserve." In the lecture titled "The Thing," "nearness" is his first and main concern.[43] The philosopher wishes to demonstrate what "nearness" is; in order to explain it, he has recourse to what is "near," i.e., "things." "But what is a thing?" Thus begins a singular analysis of "a being" that Heidegger calls "thing."

Heidegger then chooses a *particular* "thing," a "jar." As with the "thing," it is necessary to ask what the "jar" is. What then follows is an impressive "phenomenological" description that culminates in the demonstration that the "jar" gathers "earth and sky, divinities and mortals," that is to say, the "single fold of the four," i.e., the "fourfold."[44] Given that the "thing" is able to do this, we can say about its "essence" that "the thing things."[45]

Heidegger attributes other properties to the "object" and "standing reserve." The object corresponds to a "mere representation."[46] Therefore, the "object" (*Gegenstand*) is at first simply objective, an "object" that must always be the "object" of a "subject." According to Heidegger, "subject" and "object" are, since Descartes, mutually implicated in the "subject–object relation."[47] The "object" must also be distinguished from "standing reserve" (*Bestand*). The object first of all preserves, insofar as it is what "stands opposite," a certain "distance" (*Abstand*).[48] Yet this "distance" is not at all stable; it collapses into the "distanceless." All objects "slide into the basic trait of the indifferent." What is "present" is no longer experienced as an "object" but as "standing reserve." This is what occurs in the "universal requisitioning of positionality."[49]

Among the "things" at the heart of the "fourfold," Heidegger also includes plants and trees.[50] The "fourfold" is the "worlding world."[51] Since the 1920s, the philosopher had dealt with the question of the unified nexus in which Dasein relates to "beings" as the particular "beings" that they are. For Heidegger, this unified and differentiated structure is the "world," the different aspects of which he had earlier analyzed and described as "surrounding world," "shared world," "world of the self." In *Being and Time*, Heidegger considers

Dasein as "being-in-the-world." "World" is that "within" which Dasein lives.

At the same time, from this indirect reference to the specific spatiality of "world," we can deduce that the "world" which contains all things cannot be of the order of "beings." Were we to understand "world" as "a being," we would have to depict it as a kind of circumscribed container that circumscribes its content in turn. Such a hyper-object does not exist. With this insight into the non-objectivity or, to use Heidegger's term, "non-beingness" of world, the link between the "problem of being" and the problem of "world" becomes evident.[52] Although Heidegger discusses this, he does not seem prepared to relativize the "question of being." In the final analysis, "being" was for him a more original phenomenon. One reason for this may be that Platonic and Aristotelian philosophy was not aware of this "problem of world," which emerges only in the modern age, for example in Kant. Nevertheless, the fact that "world" has an ontological status, that is to say, that it is not of the order of "beings," makes clear why Heidegger remained interested in this problem.

The fact that "world" is neither simply "a being" nor identical with "being" appears to be an aporia. What can we possibly say about "world" if this concept does not articulate the relationship the particular has to the universal? If it does not say anything universal about something particular? (The notion of plural "worlds" only makes sense if we distinguish between one individual "world" and another: for example, the "world of craftsmanship." This, however, renders the "problem of world as such" incomprehensible.) Heidegger finds a way out of this aporia with the help of a tautology: "world worlds."[53] The being of the world consists, then, in the fact that it "worlds."

Heidegger very often employed this kind of tautology – for example, the "thing things." In everyday German speech, we are familiar with these kinds of tautological formulations: "the green greens" (*das Grün grünt*) or "the day days" (*der Tag tagt*). In order to avoid the repetition, these verbs are usually preceded by the German impersonal pronoun "*es*" (it). Here, what matters to Heidegger is to find a way to express the absolutely peculiar manner in which the "world" happens in a "being-like manner," even though "world" is not "being itself." Heidegger's statements in "The Origin of the Work of Art" lecture constantly testify to the proximity that exists between "world" and "being": "*World worlds*, and is more fully in being than all those tangible and perceptible things in the midst of which we take ourselves to be at home."[54] The notion of a "worlding world" that can be "more fully in being" than those tangible and perceptible "beings" belongs to the narrative of the "history of being." Certainly, the history of philosophy knows an ontological economy in which it is possible to think "being" to various degrees of intensity, for example, as in Plato's distinction between *ontos on* and *mē on*. Yet Heidegger without a doubt wants to go beyond this and think the event-like character of "world." He then tellingly adds: "Wherever the essential decisions of our history are made, wherever we take them over or abandon them, wherever they go unrecognized or are brought once more into question, there the world worlds."[55] "World" is the place of drama or tragedy. In the first instance, "world" here is not understood as the stable living space for Dasein; rather, "world" is the place where this living space becomes precarious and even shattered due to the serious nature of given political events. This is precisely why Heidegger was interested in the "factical life" of "primordial Christianity" that strives for a "total break."[56] And this was precisely what he recognized in the "national revolution" of 1933.

Heidegger systematically staged this drama: "In worlding there gathers that spaciousness from out of which the protective grace of the gods is gifted or is refused. Even the doom of the absence of the god is a way in which world worlds." In the "metapolitical" context of his thinking around 1933, Heidegger had noted that a "true appearing or non-appearing of the God in the being of the people" is necessary if a "people" is to constitute itself in the first place.[57] One of the quintessential aspects of the Heideggerian narrative of a "history of being" is to derive the "problem of world" from such a theophany and its absence.

Heidegger's formulation regarding the "worldlessness of Judaism" shows us what is problematic about this conception of "world."[58] Heidegger does not at all seem to be of the opinion that we must ascribe this "worldlessness" to Judaism as such. Rather, Heidegger attributes this worldlessness to "one of the most concealed forms of the *gigantic*, and perhaps the oldest," that is to say, "the tenacious facility in calculating, manipulating, and interfering." Thus it is "machination" that brings about the "worldlessness of Judaism." Nevertheless, it is striking that Heidegger speaks of "perhaps the oldest" "form of the gigantic." Is it not the case that Judaism perhaps plays a distinctive role in the history of "machination" since Heidegger indeed assigns to Judaism an "emphatically calculative giftedness"?[59] Be that as it may, the distinction between "worldlessness" and "worlding world" only makes sense if a certain narrative informs this concept of "world." For what can a "worlding world" be if not an event about which there is much to tell? The fact that, for Heidegger, "Judaism" or "World-Judaism" is a figure for the lack of a narrative testifies to his intention to associate Jews with calculation.

This fundamental narrative tendency also informs Heidegger's thinking of the "fourfold." The "fourfold" unites four elements, namely, the two pairs "earth and sky, divinities and mortals."[60] In German, the prefix *Ge-* characterizes a gathering of different elements that belong together. For example, a *Gebirge* (mountain range) is the gathering of different *Berge* (mountains). Therefore, Heidegger accordingly characterizes the four elements "earth and sky, divinities and mortals" as the "united four" which gather "in the single fold of their fourfold, united of themselves."

According to the philosopher, the "world" of the "fourfold" can only exist in this form of the "united four." The fact that this "world" can exist or does exist is not to be deduced from other things: the "fourfold" is "neither explicable by nor grounded upon anything other than itself." It either happens or not. Here Heidegger is pursuing an anti-metaphysical idea: "world," as the "fourfold," is not grounded in God, the subject, or even nature. It exists without ground (*grundlos*) or "abyssally" (*abgründig*).

This groundlessness poses a particular problem for the thought of the "fourfold." Heidegger has to explain the "fourfold" solely on its own terms. Over the course of his explanation, he accomplishes this by combining phenomenological and narratival elements. Heidegger initially stresses that, though it is possible to analyze each of the fourfold's "elements" one by one, each element cannot be "thought" in isolation from the others. As concerns the "earth," this is expressed in the following way: "When we say earth then we already think, in case we are thinking, the other three along with it from the single fold of the fourfold."[61] "Earth" is only itself when it relates to "sky, divinities and mortals." This is a phenomenological suggestion that the "earth" itself confirms. As the philosopher says, the "earth" can only be "what nourishingly fructifies" because it receives rain from the "sky." The tales of the "divinities" are linked to this fruitfulness. Heidegger is thinking here of Hölderlin's hymn "Mother Earth." One way "mortals" relate to the "earth" is by the fact that they will be buried in it (in a Christian context, at any rate). Not a single one of the "four elements" can ever be "thought" without the "other three." The same goes for all the elements. In the "fourfold," the four elements always appear as four and mutually reflect each other; this is why Heidegger designates this relational totality with the term "mirror-play."[62]

The "divinities and mortals" pair most clearly demonstrates why it is that the "fourfold" ultimately articulates a narratival concept of "world." Heidegger specifies that the divinities are "hinting messengers of godhood."[63] From this point of view, the figure of the angel orients the philosopher. According to Christianity, angels (*angelloi*) are "messengers" who exist between mortals and gods and who announce God's plan, e.g., the conception and birth of Jesus Christ. Heidegger, however, describes them as "hinting messengers." A "hint" gestures toward what is concealed or what is yet to come. This is what "godhood" is for Heidegger. That being said, this "godhood" is not "the god" itself but rather something like the dimension in which "the god" can appear in the first place. Thus, Heidegger writes, "From the concealed reign of these there appears the god in his essence, withdrawing him from every comparison with what is present."[64] "The god" is not the same thing as "the divine." The latter first prepares the coming of the former. We can see that an eschatological narrative also holds sway in the "fourfold."

Heidegger's account of "mortals" corroborates this point. In his later thinking, Heidegger substitutes the concept of "mortals" for that of "*Da-sein*." Since *Being and Time*, "being-toward-death" was for Heidegger one of Dasein's most important "ways of being." Moreover, Greek tragedy oriented Heidegger's displacement of "*Da-sein*" into the notion of "mortals." Beginning with the myths of the oracle at Delphi, Greek tragedy grasped the human being as the *thnētos* or *brotos*, that is to say, as a mortal being as opposed to the gods. Plato, and Aristotle to an even greater extent, both rejected these tragic notions of the human being, which prompted Heidegger to take them up in his own thinking.

For Heidegger, the fact that human beings are "mortals" does not mean that they must die in this or that way; rather, it means that "they are capable of death as death." As already is the case in *Being and Time*, this notion allows us to consider death as a positive possibility of existence. We "can" die, but not in the sense of *ars moriendi*; rather, we "can" die in the sense of being open for death. Heidegger wants to hear the verb *mögen* (to like) in *vermögen* (to be able to); it then becomes clear that this sense of death constitutes the "essence" of the human being, an "essence" that the human being "likes" because that is who the human is.

According to Heidegger, however, history shows us that the human being is by no means "able" to die. In the second Bremen lecture on "positionality," Heidegger writes: "Hundreds of thousands die in masses. Do they die? They perish. They are put down. Do they die? They become pieces of inventory of a standing reserve for the fabrication of corpses. Do they die? They are unobtrusively liquidated in annihilation camps. And even apart from such as these – millions now in China abjectly end in starvation."[65]

The genocide of the Shoah – something hardly "unobtrusive" in every respect imaginable – is the paradigm of a conception of the human being that Heidegger's discourse on "mortals" opposes. For the philosopher, "death in masses" is a "horrific undying death."[66] Here, the crime consists not only in the annihilation of life, but of death as well. Many people shared the view that a concentration camp took away not just the life but also the death of those who died. For example, in his account "The Death of My Father," Elie Wiesel writes, "His death did not even belong to him. I do not know to what cause to attribute it, in what book to inscribe it. No link between it and the life he had led. His death, lost in the masses, had nothing to do with the individual he had been."[67]

For Heidegger, the "fabrication of corpses" is an indication that the human being is "not yet the mortal."[68] This has, however, important consequences for the "fourfold." Its structure remains incomplete as long as "mortals" do not yet exist. This leads to the question of whether the same thing can also be said of "earth, sky, and the divinities." What is the actual status of the "fourfold"?

The first of the Bremen Lectures begins with a discussion on the "*thing*," i.e., the "fourfold." The second lecture deals with "positionality." As Heidegger denies the possibility that human beings are "mortals," he makes clear that there is no "fourfold" in "positionality." At the heart of "positionality" is "standing reserve," but not "the thing" which gathers the "fourfold." How do "positionality" and the "fourfold" relate to each other? "Fourfold" is the "world" in which the "recovery of technology," i.e., the "recovery" of the "fourfold," has taken place. "Positionality" blocks, or perhaps even denies, our access to "world." Something that is denied is not impossible: no wonder, then, that Heidegger suggests that, "presumably suddenly, the world can world as world one more time."[69]

The "fourfold" participates in the "mytho-logy of the event of appropriation"; it is a "poetized world." Even "positionality" is a mythological figure, especially when we consider how it relates to the "fourfold." And yet, "How can one know what history is if one does not know what poetry is [...]?"[70] But is it really the case that "history" discloses itself only when it is expressed in "poetic" language? Since the discovery of the "history of being" in the beginning of the 1930s, this sentence has watched over the whole of Heidegger's thought, in particular everything he had to say after World War I. It is "poetry" in the broadest sense, i.e., a thoroughly poetic perspective on philosophical problems, which made Heidegger's thought so productive. It is not simply the case that poetry set Heidegger on his "paths," his wayward and "errant" paths; rather, the very notion that thought is a "path" that may "go astray" is *itself* poetically inflected.

The question is whether and how a narratival thinking of this kind can be at all relevant to twentieth- and twenty-first-century philosophy. Today, the prevailing moderate tone of philosophical discourse appears to rely on a rigorous distinction between myth and philosophy. Is it even possible for myth to be a contemporary topic? Thus we may predict what will be left of Heidegger: *Being and Time* and the lecture courses that either paved the way for Heidegger's magnum opus or came after it. This, however, is only a historiographical fact that belongs in a museum. In one of his latest texts, Heidegger says the following: "The awakening to the event of appropriation must be experienced, it cannot be proven."[71] Philosophy must go beyond its historiographical means of communication. This can only happen when someone starts to philosophize. Perhaps this beginning – which cannot be confused either with the "first" or with the "other" inception – follows a poetic impulse. Over and beyond their merely historiographical transmission, Heidegger's works leave us with the thought that, in philosophy, one must always begin again.

5

Reverberations

The impact of Heidegger's philosophy on the intellectual climate in Europe – and, beyond Europe, the entire world – was immense. He is one of the most translated German philosophers. Without his work, we cannot understand contemporary French philosophy.[1] Though it is true that Heidegger's thought has had more of an impact in certain fields (such as literary criticism) and less so in others (such as history), not a single discipline in the humanities escapes its influence. This also results from the fact that Heidegger had a great many students, men and women who went on to become extremely influential in turn.

One particular chapter in the history of the reception of Heidegger's thought is the way in which analytic philosophy relates to this type of thinking and its followers. A good example of the enormous difficulties (from both sides) that prevent a rapprochement is Rudolf Carnap's essay "The Overcoming of Metaphysics Through the Logical Analysis of Language," which had been published in 1932. Taking select sentences from Heidegger and Hegel as his point of departure, Carnap's essay shows how this type of thinking is "meaningless."[2] According to Carnap, the statements Heidegger and Hegel make always get entangled in peculiar "language cases" that never correspond to the empirical facts of empirical sciences. This is why, for Carnap, this type of thinking is not simply "mere speculation" or a bunch of "fairy tales" but rather a "phraseology" of "pseudo-statements." The latter amounts to no more than the "general attitude of a person toward life." Carnap thus describes thinkers like Hegel, Nietzsche, or Heidegger as "musicians without musical ability." It is nearly impossible to surmount the philosophical divide that exists between Heidegger and Carnap. Therefore, very rarely do we find Heideggerian work in the present context of "philosophy of mind."

Hans-Georg Gadamer was one of Heidegger's students during his Marburg period. In his 1960 magnum opus *Truth and Method*, Gadamer develops a "phenomenological hermeneutics," the term Heidegger still used in *Being and Time* to describe the core of his method. *Truth and Method* was highly influential during the 1960s for the human sciences as a whole. In his "hermeneutics," however, Gadamer no longer considers the interpretation of texts to be merely a method. For Gadamer, the act of philosophizing is itself a "conversation" with our "tradition." The latter does not appear as a clear textual corpus. Instead, following a Heideggerian intuition, Gadamer argues that we must "hermeneutically experience" our tradition.[3] Heidegger's interpretation of a "facticity of life" that becomes transparent to itself in "authenticity" reappears in the notion of an "authentic experience" that amounts to the experience of one's own "historicity."

Though not always clearly discernible as such, Heidegger's philosophy is omnipresent in the writings of Jacques Derrida. In the context of "writing," "text," and "language," Derrida sheds light on the metaphysically determined notions of "logocentrism" and "phonocentrism" that *necessarily* distort the original sense of "writing" and "text."[4] This more original sense of "writing" is not to be understood as a ground or principle. Rather, "writing" must be thought of in terms of a ground that rejects every ground, i.e., in terms of *différance* – in the two senses of the French verb *différer* ("to defer" and "to differ"). Even though Heidegger's thinking largely remains trapped in the history of "logocentrism," his philosophy also describes the "closure" (*clôture*) of an epoch from which thought cannot escape even as it simultaneously leaves this epoch behind. For Derrida, the project of "deconstructing" this epoch dismantles the significations that conceal *différance*, the same *différance* that makes deconstruction possible in the first place. For Derrida, this "deconstruction" has an ethical sense.

Emmanuel Levinas once expressed in an interview his "admiration and disappointment" in relation to Heidegger's thought.[5] He emphasizes that, with Heidegger, the "'verbal character' of the term 'being' was revived." For Heidegger, this event-like quality of "being" was what he called the "event of appropriation." The specific link between "the meaning of the term 'being' as a verb" and Levinas's thinking stems from the fact that Heidegger's thought steers phenomenology away from Husserl's "transcendental program" in order to discover, by means of the temporality of "being," the ground that makes possible practical questions and experiences. It might be possible to link Heidegger's repeated attempt to think the "event of appropriation" in terms of the back-and-forth of two *relata* to Levinas's central thought that the "self" of the "subject" is first constituted by the "claim" of the "other." Yet we must stress that, apart from the analysis of "being-with" in *Being and Time*, Heidegger's thought not only entirely dismisses the concept of the "other" as such but also blocks access to it. "Being" ignores the "claim" of the "other." This is what Levinas shows in the essay "Heidegger, Gagarin and Us."[6]

Hannah Arendt, one of Heidegger's students and early mistresses, is very close to his philosophy of technology, especially in her important book from 1958 titled *The Human Condition*.[7] Heidegger's philosophy also seems to have influenced Arendt's writings on the Shoah, such as, for example, her first major work *The Origins of Totalitarianism* (1951). It may well be that some of the insights Arendt gleaned from Heidegger influenced the stark critique she puts forth in *Eichmann in Jerusalem*, one of her later texts in which she transposed a number of these Heideggerian ideas.[8]

In 1964, Theodor W. Adorno published his critical text *The Jargon of Authenticity*. The title refers to Heidegger's discussion of "authenticity" in *Being and Time*. In a warning tone, Adorno writes: "In Germany a jargon of authenticity is spoken – even more so, written. Its language is a trademark of societalized chosenness, noble and homey at once – sublanguage as superior language."[9] Adorno criticizes Heidegger's thought for being extremely "provincial" and for believing

in "immediacy," an "ideology as language, without any consideration of specific content."[10] Adorno aims his criticism
not just at Heidegger but also at Otto F. Bollnow and even
Karl Jaspers. Beyond these objections belonging to the critique
of ideology, Adorno arrives at philosophical considerations
when he establishes that "through the jargon of authenticity,"
the "underlying experiences of metaphysics are simply degraded
as a habit of thought which sublimates them into metaphysical
suffering and cuts them off from the actual suffering it pro-
vokes"; "the entire hatred of jargon" goes "against the consciousness of this suffering."[11] In fact, there is in Heidegger
a peculiar indifference with respect to the "actual suffering"
of human beings.

Günther Anders was a student of Heidegger between 1921
and 1924. It was only in 2001 that his critical notes were
published, which show that Anders engaged intensively with
his teacher's thinking for decades. Like Levinas, Anders is
critical of the fact that, although Heidegger decisively revital-
ized twentieth-century philosophy, his thought nevertheless
neglects certain ethical and political aspects of human existence.
Thus, by fixating on "*the* Dasein," argues Anders, Heidegger
did not take the plurality of human freedom into account.[12]
In addition, Anders calls attention to a blindness in Heidegger's
philosophy to the basic human need for a body. Why does
Heidegger speak of "thrownness" in *Being and Time* if, for
example, "hunger" drives every Dasein? According to Anders,
Heidegger's later work reveals itself to be "linguistic esoteri-
cism" and a "philosophy of piety."

In *The Destruction of Reason*, Georg Lukács offers a
Marxist-Leninist reading of Heidegger. Lukács has some interesting things to say about the "elementary historicity of
Dasein."[13] To see this as "the basis for comprehending history"
turns out to be, according to Lukács, "pure shadow-boxing."[14]
For Heidegger, "Dasein is the original phenomenon of history";
from this Lukács mistakenly concludes that the context of
"lived experience" is the foundation of "historicity." A double
"distortion" results from this: first, Heidegger allegedly does
not recognize the "historical facts in nature" as part of the
"original phenomenon of history." Second, Heidegger does
not realize that his "original phenomenon" is a "consequence
of the being of society, of the social praxis of human beings."

Being and Time is related to "the spiritual conditions prompted by the crisis of postwar imperialistic capitalism."[15] There is one thing Lukács gets right. Heidegger never accepted the Marxist distinction between infrastructure and superstructure. "Social being" always had to be transformed into a narrative. Were this "social being" to appear as such, Heidegger would have considered it as "ahistorical."

We should not underestimate the influence Heidegger's philosophy has on the writings of Peter Sloterdijk. This influence can be seen, above all, in a collection of his essays titled *Not Saved: Essays After Heidegger*. In a prefatory note, Sloterdijk writes:

> Heidegger's accomplishment – and because of it the indispensability of his voice in the conversation of the present age with the future – in my opinion consists in the fact that, under the title of the question of Being, he worked for his entire life on a logic of commitment that, even before the division of ontology and ethics, remained on the trail of the antagonism between liberating and compulsory tendencies in the Dasein of those who die and those who are born.[16]

Sloterdijk's "logic of commitment" is that "responsive" structure which Heidegger, taking the "ontological difference" as his point of departure, attempted to explain in the central figures of his thought. Heidegger's thought is unrelentingly interested in the "event of appropriation of the re-lation" and seeks it out everywhere possible.[17]

Jean-Luc Nancy follows a similar ethical strand in his essay "Heidegger's 'Originary Ethics.'"[18] According to Nancy, "Only those who have read Heidegger blindly, or not at all, have been able to think of him as a stranger to ethical preoccupations."[19] Nancy explains that an ethical action such as Heidegger thinks it arises from "Being's propriety of sense – which consists precisely in a having-to-make-sense, and not in the disposition of a given *proper sense*."[20] Nihilism appears then as a "general dissolution of sense." And Nancy explains that "thinking, in its sense of 'original ethics,' is the experience of this absolute responsibility for sense."[21]

Though very little attention has been paid to it, there is much to be said about Heidegger's influence on "media studies," particularly on the work of Friedrich Kittler who founded a

new approach to media studies. Kittler's work on the history
and theory of media moved him closer and closer to Heideggerian philosophy, which he takes up in an entirely affirmative
manner. Heidegger scholarship has yet to appreciate this reception of Heidegger's thought – which is not the case for the
scholarship on Kittler.[22]

One singular aspect of the historical reception of Heidegger's
thinking is the influence he had on poets. His thought had
particular impact not only on the relationship between Paul
Celan and Ingeborg Bachmann – who wrote a dissertation on
Heidegger in 1949 – but on Celan himself. In the 1950s,
Heidegger would send his publications to Celan, who read
everything carefully. In 1967, Heidegger wrote the following
to Gerhart Baumann: "I know everything about him; I know,
too, what a serious crisis he went through, which he pulled
himself out of as much as a man is able."[23] The same year,
Celan visited Heidegger in Todtnauberg. A like-named poem
("Todtnauberg") was the result of this visit, which has taken
on a mythical status.[24] In the draft of an undated letter, Celan
writes:

Heidegger
... that you (by your stance) have decisively weakened that
which is poetic and, I venture to surmise, that which is thinking, in the serious responsibility to both.[25]

When Botho Strauß's essay "Swelling Goat Song" appeared
in 1993, an indignation surfaced in the press that just as
quickly disappeared. In this essay, Strauß established a link
with the thinking of Heidegger and Ernst Jünger. He writes:
"They put Heidegger on the index and suspected Jünger – now
they must accept that the great strides made by these authors,
poet-philosophers, trample underfoot, like a dried thistle abandoned along the way, their well-intentioned rebellion."[26] Later,
Strauß would again engage with Heidegger's poetry, published
in volume 81 of the *Gesamtausgabe*. He points out that this
poetry "submits communicational intelligence to a trial by
fire."[27] It is also at the same time a "fire that ravages a pile
of circumstantial garbage": it produces a purification.

In an interview from 1986, Peter Handke admits that he
wishes to "introduce or adapt the term 'world' in such a place

[...], to find for it a place [...] where it might emerge from the shadows and come back into the light." He sees the same gesture in Heidegger who "made this extraordinary attempt."[28] However, Handke simultaneously takes his distance from the overly "poetic configuration" of words in Heidegger's statements. Some of Handke's statements resonate with Heidegger's thinking; yet, when Handke uses nearly identical formulations, something else is at stake:

> A crossing of the river takes shape in the form of a bridge; a stretch of water becomes a lake; the walker felt he was continuously accompanied by a chain of hills, a row of houses, an orchard; the container surrounded by something living where what was common to all these things was this unappearance that is close to the heart, a general belonging to the world: the real which, precisely, makes possible nothing other than the feeling of being at home, that "Here I am at last!"[29]

The publication of the first nineteen volumes of the *Black Notebooks* in 2014 is a decisive event in the history of the reception of Heidegger's philosophy. At stake there are less Heidegger's statements that testify to his proximity to – and his distancing from – National Socialism, than his use of anti-Semitic stereotypes in the context of a narrative in the "history of being." In 1989, Victor Farías's book *Heidegger and National Socialism* gave rise to the first international discussion on this problematic theme.[30] However, due to peculiar errors in Farías's interpretation of Heidegger, his work ultimately had no repercussions on the reception of Heidegger's philosophy. In 2005, with the publication of Emmanuel Faye's *Heidegger: The Introduction of Nazism into Philosophy*, the discussions on Heidegger's wayward political paths made a qualitative leap. In this work, Faye advances a position that the publication of the *Black Notebooks* would appear to confirm. For Faye, "far from enriching philosophy," Heidegger "has worked to destroy it, by making it subservient to a movement that, by the murderous discrimination underlying it and the project of collective annihilation to which it leads, constitutes the radical negation of all humanity and all thought."[31] However, as was the case in Farías, Faye's unnecessary speculations weaken his interpretation. For example, "It is [...] not absurd to formulate the hypothesis that among the hidden networks of Nazism, which we still know so little about today, Heidegger might have played a certain role in the preliminary conception of Hitler's speeches" – a thesis that cannot be proven by any supporting evidence.[32]

In 2010, Holger Zaborowski published his meticulous work *A Question of Error and Guilt? Martin Heidegger and National Socialism*.[33] The author reacts to Faye's simplistic argument by introducing a complication. It very quickly becomes clear when we consider this issue "how complex the question of Heidegger's relationship to National Socialism really is." "In the final analysis, there is not simply just *one* question concerning this relationship." Therefore, whoever decides to "really take up this issue in a philosophical or historical way will soon realize that a simple answer will not do, and that, though many questions are now answerable, just as many others remain open." In the meantime, these positions have been surpassed by Donatella di Cesare's interpretations in her book *Heidegger and the Jews* where she speaks of a "metaphysical anti-Semitism" that Heidegger shares with a number of philosophers such as Kant, Fichte, Hegel, and Nietzsche.[34] With his anti-Semitism, Heidegger would remain trapped in the metaphysics which he nevertheless claims to overcome. There is still an ongoing debate on Heidegger's *Black Notebooks*. The national and international reverberations generated by their publication demonstrate that Heidegger's thought still occupies a central place in the general and public interest in philosophy.

Biographical Facts in
Historical Context

Life – my life, your life, their life, we want to get to know
the most general aspects of our life and, indeed, in such a
way that we remain in life, looking around us in accordance
with *the way of life*.[1]

September 9 1889 Martin Heidegger is born in Meßkirch, a
small town in the region of Baden-Württemberg. He would
go on to develop an intimate relationship with this town
located north of Lake Constance, at the southwestern edge
of the Alps. In the same year, Ludwig Wittgenstein is born
on April 26 and Adolf Hitler on April 20.

1909–1911 Heidegger studies theology and philosophy at the
University of Freiburg. Gustav Mahler dies in Vienna. In
Berlin, Arnold Schönberg composes the *Six Little Piano
Pieces, op. 19*. In 1910, Rainer Maria Rilke publishes *The
Notebooks of Malte Laurids Brigge*.

1911–1913 At the University of Freiburg, Heidegger studies
philosophy and delves into the human and natural sciences.
In 1912, Ernest Rutherford develops the atomic model.

1913 Heidegger writes his PhD dissertation under Arthur
Schneider in Freiburg. The *Armory Show* art exhibition takes

place in New York. Artists such as Marcel Duchamp, Pablo Picasso, and Kazimir Malevich display their works in the United States for the first time. In Detroit, Henry Ford installs the first moving assembly line. Igor Stravinsky's *Rite of Spring* is premiered in Paris, a performance that became one of the greatest scandals in music history.

1914 World War I erupts. On March 11, Georg Trakl dies in a military hospital in Krakow. Heidegger publishes his dissertation titled *The Doctrine of Judgment in Psychologism: A Critical and Positive Contribution to Logic*. From the end of 1915 until the beginning of 1918, he serves in the German army as a postal censor in Freiburg. In 1918, from the end of August until the beginning of November, he serves as a weather forecaster in the Warfront Meteorology Corps 414 of the Third Army.

1915 Under Heinrich Rickert, Heidegger writes his qualifying dissertation – published in 1916 – on *Duns Scotus' Theories of the Categories and of Meaning*. Albert Einstein publishes his theory of general relativity.

1916 Heidegger publishes the essay "The Concept of Time in History." In England, Tritton and Wilson invent the tank.

1917 Heidegger marries Elfride Petri. The October Revolution takes place in Saint Petersburg.

1918 Heidegger is promoted to lance corporal. On November 9, Philipp Scheidemann proclaims the end of Germany's monarchy from one of the windows of the Reichstag building.

1919 Heidegger becomes Husserl's personal assistant at the University of Freiburg. His first son Jörg is born on January 21.

1920 Hermann, his second (non-biological) son, who would later become the first literary executor of the Heidegger estate, is born on August 20. In Leipzig, Ernst Jünger self-publishes *Storm of Steel*. On November 23, Paul Celan is born in Czernowitz.

1922 The Heideggers move to the hut (*die Hütte*) – planned and designed by Elfride herself – in Todtnauberg, in the south of the Black Forest. In London, Wittgenstein publishes the *Tractatus Logico-Philosophicus*. On October 31, Benito Mussolini seizes power in Italy.

1923 As an *ad personam* full professor, Heidegger is called to an associate professorship at the University of Marburg. Rilke publishes *The Duino Elegies*. On November 8–9, the Beer Hall Putsch fails in Munich.

1924 Hannah Arendt begins to study with Heidegger in Marburg. Vladimir Ilyich Lenin dies in Gorki, near Moscow.

1926 The second volume of Hitler's *Mein Kampf* is published in Munich; the first volume had appeared in 1925. Rilke dies on December 29 near Montreux, on Lake Geneva. On June 1, Norma Jean Baker (alias Marilyn Monroe) is born in Los Angeles.

1927 *Being and Time* is published in the *Yearbook for Philosophy and Phenomenological Research*. On October 1, Heidegger becomes chair of philosophy at Marburg University. Fritz Lang releases the film *Metropolis*.

1928 Heidegger becomes Husserl's successor at the University of Freiburg. The Heideggers move into a house designed by Elfride, located at Rötebuckweg 47 in Zähringen, a suburb of Freiburg. Stefan George publishes his last poem, "The Kingdom Come." On October 6, Andy Warhol is born in Pittsburgh.

1929 Heidegger delivers the lecture titled "What is Metaphysics?," his inaugural address as a professor at the University of Freiburg which is then published in the same year. He simultaneously publishes *Kant and the Problem of Metaphysics* and the essay "On the Essence of Ground" in a Festschrift celebrating Edmund Husserl's seventieth birthday. In the United States, Vladimir Zworykin invents the kinescope television system. Heidegger and Cassirer debate Kant in Davos.

1930 Heidegger turns down a position in Berlin for the first time. The Nazi Party (NSDAP) becomes the second-strongest party in Germany after the Social Democratic Party (SPD). Jacques Derrida is born on July 15 in El Biar, Algeria. In New York, Max Schmeling becomes the World Heavyweight Champion for the first time on June 12.

1931 In Berlin, Ernst Ruska and Max Knoll design the first electron microscope. Heidegger begins writing the manuscript of *Ponderings*, the first volumes of the *Black Notebooks*.

1933 Hitler is appointed Chancellor of the Reich. By an almost unanimous vote, Heidegger is elected rector of Freiburg University. He joins the Nazi Party. In May, he delivers the Rectorial Address titled "The Self-Assertion of the German University." In his summer semester lecture course of that year, he deals with "The Fundamental Question of Philosophy." He turns down a second offer for a position in Berlin and another one in Munich. On December 4, Stefan George dies in Minusio on the northern shore of Lake Maggiore, in the district of Locarno, Switzerland. Hannah Arendt emigrates to Paris.

1934 Heidegger steps down from the rectorship. In the winter semester of 1934–5, he gives the lecture course titled "Hölderlin's Hymns 'Germania' and 'The Rhine.'" On July 6, the leader of the Sturmabteilung Party (SA) is murdered – the so-called Röhm Putsch.

1935 In the summer semester, Heidegger gives the lecture course titled "Introduction to Metaphysics." The Nuremberg Laws are introduced. On December 1, Woody Allen is born in Brooklyn, New York.

1936 Heidegger publishes the essay "Hölderlin and the Essence of Poetry." In the winter semester of 1936–7, he gives the first lecture course on Nietzsche titled "Nietzsche: The Will to Power as Art." He starts working on *Contributions to Philosophy (Of the Event)*, which is published only in 1989. The first functional helicopter, the Focke-Wulf Fw 61, is invented in Bremen. Berlin hosts the Summer Olympics. Alan

Turing invents the Turing machine. On February 5, Charlie Chaplin's film *Modern Times* is released in the United States.

1937 The Condor Legion bombs Guernica; Picasso starts working on a painting by the same name. In Nanking, the Japanese army massacres the Chinese people during the Second Sino-Japanese War. Walt Disney releases *Snow White and the Seven Dwarfs*.

1938 Husserl dies in Freiburg on April 27. In November, the Night of the Broken Glass takes place. The synagogue right next to the University of Freiburg is burned down. In New York, the photocopier is invented.

1939 World War II begins.

1940 Heidegger delivers lectures on Ernst Jünger's *The Worker* to a small group of colleagues at the University of Freiburg. Jünger himself does his military service as a squadron commander at Westwall. In October, Jews in Freiburg are deported to the French concentration camp in Gurs. On October 9, John Lennon is born in Liverpool.

1941 Heidegger publishes the essay "Hölderlin's Hymn 'As When on a Holiday'." The Auschwitz Concentration Camp is built. The Messerschmitt 262, the world's first jet-powered fighter aircraft, is invented in Augsburg. In Berlin, Konrad Zuse builds the Z3, the first operational computer. Hannah Arendt arrives in New York.

1942 On January 10, fifteen high-ranking Nazi Party officials meet in Wannsee to discuss the Final Solution to the Jewish Question. Heidegger gives a lecture course on Hölderlin's hymn "Remembrance." He publishes "Plato's Doctrine of Truth." The film *Die grosse Lieber* (*The Great Love*, with Zarah Leander), the most successful German film to date, is released. On December 6, Peter Handke is born in Griffen, Austria.

1943 The Soviets destroy the Sixth Army in Stalingrad. Heidegger publishes the lecture "On the Essence of Truth." On

November 30, Terrence Malick, the translator of Heidegger's "On the Essence of Ground" and director of the film *The Thin Red Line*, is born in Waco, Texas.

1944 The Western Allies land in Normandy. In November, Heidegger is drafted into the *Volkssturm* national militia and is then released one month later. Aerial attacks destroy most of Freiburg's historic district. Claus von Stauffenberg's assassination plot against Hitler fails on July 20. A former student of Stefan George, von Stauffenberg is executed in Berlin on July 21.

1945 On January 27, the Red Army liberates Auschwitz. Hitler dies and Germany unconditionally surrenders. The Denazification Committee recommends that Heidegger be given an emeritus status with the "possibility of limited teaching." His family residence is confiscated. His sons Hermann and Jörg are captured by the Soviets. The American airforce drops the atomic bomb on Hiroshima and Nagasaki. Franz Beckenbauer is born on September 11.

1946 From time to time, Heidegger seeks psychological treatment in Badenweiler. The Senate of Freiburg University recommends that he be given emeritus status without permission to teach. The French occupying power also bans Heidegger from teaching. He meets Jean Beaufret for the first time. On October 16, twelve major German war criminals, including Alfred Rosenberg and Julius Streicher, are executed in Nuremberg.

1948 Norbert Wiener publishes *Cybernetics: Or Control and Communication in the Animal and the Machine*.

1947 Heidegger publishes the so-called "Letter on Humanism," together with the older essay "Plato's Doctrine of Truth." The Soviets release his younger son Hermann and he comes home. Thomas Mann publishes *Doctor Faustus*. Arnold Schönberg composes *A Survivor from Warsaw, op. 46*.

1949 The French authorities lift Heidegger's teaching ban. He delivers the Bremen Lectures. The Soviets release his son

Jörg and he also comes home. On October 1, Mao Zedong proclaims the People's Republic of China.

1950 Heidegger starts receiving a pension and meets Hannah Arendt again. He publishes *Off the Beaten Track*. The Japanese film *Rashomon* directed by Akira Kurosawa is released.

1951 He is given emeritus status. In the winter semester of 1951–2, and in the following summer, he gives his last major lecture course titled "What is Called Thinking?," which is then published in 1954. On July 13, Schönberg dies in Los Angeles.

1952 Paul Celan publishes *Poppy and Memory*.

1953 On March 5, Stalin dies near Moscow.

1954 Heidegger publishes *Lectures and Conferences*. In Bern, Germany wins the World Cup for the first time. The first nuclear power plant is set up in Obninsk, USSR.

1955 At Cerisy-la-Salle, Normandy, Heidegger delivers the lecture "Qu'est-ce que la philosophie?," which is then published a year later. Beaufret organized the event. Glenn Gould plays Bach's *Goldberg Variations* for the first time.

1957 In Baikonur, the Soviets launch *Sputnik 1* into orbit. Space travel begins.

1958 In Germany, Hannah Arendt publishes *The Origins of Totalitarianism*. Heidegger records the lecture "Identity and Difference."

1959 Heidegger publishes *On the Way to Language* and *Gelassenheit*. In Munich, he delivers his last major lecture on Hölderlin titled "Hölderlin's Earth and Sky." The Cuban Revolution is successful. Miles Davis releases the album *Kind of Blue*.

1961 Heidegger publishes *Nietzsche, Vols I and II*. The Berlin Wall is built. Adolf Eichmann, arrested in Argentina by the

Israeli secret service one year before, is sentenced to death in Jerusalem. Hannah Arendt covers the trial as a correspondent of *The New Yorker*. In 1964, her book *Eichmann in Jerusalem: A Report on the Banality of Evil* is published in Germany. Ornette Coleman records the album *Free Jazz: A Collective Improvisation*.

1962 In Freiburg, Heidegger delivers the lecture "Time and Being," which is then published in *Zur Sache des Denkens* in 1969. Heidegger and Elfride make their first trip to Greece. The first English translation of *Being and Time* by John Macquarrie and Edward Robinson is published in New York. On August 5, Marilyn Monroe commits suicide in Brentwood, Los Angeles. In October, the Cuban Missile Crisis takes place: It is suspected that the Soviets have installed middle-range ballistic missiles in Cuba. Heidegger purchases a Grundig tube radio (type 88) in order to catch up on the world's news from Todtnauberg. Andy Warhol paints *Campbell's Soup Cans*.

1965 The first sentences of the so-called *Auschwitzprozessen* ("The Frankfurt Auschwitz Trials") are issued.

1966 Heidegger gives his first seminar in Le Thor, a seminar that turned out to be extremely important for the reception of his thought in France. He meets René Char. Giorgio Agamben is one of the seminar's participants.

1967 In Athens, Heidegger speaks about "The Origin of Art and the Destinal Calling of Thinking." He meets Paul Celan in Todtnauberg. The Beatles release the album *Sgt. Pepper's Lonely Hearts Club Band*. On June 2, the student Benno Ohnesorg is shot in West Berlin. Kurt Cobain is born on February 2.

1969 On July 21, Neil Armstrong is the first man to walk on the moon. Heidegger publishes "Art and Space."

1970 Probably on April 20, Paul Celan takes his life by jumping into the Seine. Andreas Baader and Ulrike Meinhof co-found the terrorist organization the Red Army Faction.

On September 18, Jimi Hendrix dies in London. On June 17, Franz Beckenbauer and Germany's national soccer team are eliminated in the World Cup semifinals in Mexico, after losing the so-called "game of the century" to Italy by 4–3 during extra time.

1975 The *Gesamtausgabe* volumes begin to be published. Pink Floyd releases the album *Wish You Were Here*.

1976 On May 25, Heidegger dies in his own house in Zähringen, Freiburg. On May 8 or 9, Ulrike Meinhof hangs herself in her cell in the Stammheim Prison in Stuttgart. On April 1, Steve Jobs and Steve Wozniak found the company Apple.

Notes

Preface to the English Edition

1 Peter Trawny, *Heidegger and the Myth of a Jewish World Conspiracy*, trans. Andrew Mitchell (Chicago, IL: University of Chicago Press, 2015).

2 Cf. Jean-Luc Nancy, *The Banality of Heidegger*, trans. Jeff Fort (New York: Fordham University Press, 2017).

Introduction

1 Friedrich Nietzsche, "Schopenhauer as Educator," in *Untimely Meditations*, trans. R. Hollingdale, ed. Daniel Breazeale (Cambridge: Cambridge University Press, 1997), 136.

2 Martin Heidegger, *Frühe Schriften* (GA 1), ed. Friedrich-Wilhelm von Herrmann (Frankfurt am Main: Vittorio Klostermann, 1978), 437.

3 Martin Heidegger, *Holzwege* (GA 5), ed. Friedrich-Wilhelm von Herrmann (Frankfurt am Main: Vittorio Klostermann, 2003 [1977]), and *Wegmarken* (GA 9), ed. Friedrich-Wilhelm von Herrmann (Frankfurt am Main: Vittorio Klostermann, 2004 [1976]); *Off the Beaten Track*, ed. and trans. Julian Young and Kenneth Haynes (Cambridge: Cambridge University Press, 2002), and *Pathmarks*, ed. William McNeill (Cambridge: Cambridge University Press, 1998). I have provided, when available, English translations of Heidegger as they currently exist in published form, only occasionally modifying them as need be. For cases where a published English

translation does not yet exist, I have provided my own translation. Both German and English texts are fully cited once and then in the standard abbreviated form throughout: GA and the volume number followed by the German and English pagination indicated in this order [Trans.].

4 Martin Heidegger, *Unterwegs zur Sprache* (GA 12), ed. Friedrich-Wilhelm von Herrmann (Frankfurt am Main: Vittorio Klostermann, 2018 [1959]); *On the Way to Language*, trans. Peter Hertz (New York: Harper & Row, 1971).

5 Martin Heidegger, "Der Feldweg," in *Aus der Erfahrung des Denkens 1910–1976* (GA 13), ed. Hermann Heidegger (Frankfurt am Main: Vittorio Klostermann, 1983); "The Pathway," trans. Thomas F. O'Meara, revised by Thomas Sheehan, *Listening 8* (1973): 32–9.

6 Martin Heidegger, "Eine gefährliche Irrnis," in *Jahresgabe der Martin-Heidegger-Gesellschaft* (2008), 11. See too Peter Trawny, *Irrnisfuge: Heideggers An-archie* (Berlin: Matthes & Seitz, 2014); *Freedom to Fail: Heidegger's Anarchy*, trans. Ian Moore and Christopher Turner (Cambridge: Polity Press, 2015).

7 Martin Heidegger, *Der Anfang der abendländischen Philosophie. Auslegung des Anaximander und Parmenides* (GA 35), ed. Peter Trawny (Frankfurt am Main: Vittorio Klostermann, 2012), 83; *The Beginning of Western Philosophy: Interpretations of Anaximander and Parmenides*, trans. Richard Rojcewicz (Bloomington, IN: Indiana University Press, 2015), 63.

8 GA 12: 186/92 [translation modified].

9 *Martin Heidegger im Gespräch*, ed. Richard Wisser (Freiburg: Alber, 1970), 13.

10 Martin Heidegger, *Überlegungen VII–XI (Schwarze Hefte 1931–38)* (GA 95), ed. Peter Trawny (Frankfurt am Main: Vittorio Klostermann, 2014), 16; *Ponderings VII–XI, Black Notebooks 1938–1939*, trans. Richard Rojcewicz (Bloomington, IN: Indiana University Press, 2017), 13.

11 Hans-Georg Gadamer, "Ausgewählte Briefe an Martin Heidegger," in *Jahresgabe der Martin-Heidegger-Gesellschaft* (2002), 43.

12 Martin Heidegger, "Was heisst Denken," *Vorträge und Aufsätze* (GA 7), ed. Friedrich-Wilhelm von Herrmann (Frankfurt am Main: Vittorio Klostermann, 2000), 133; "What is Called Thinking?," in *Basic Writings*, ed. David Farrell Krell (New York: Harper Collins, 1993), 264.

13 Martin Heidegger, *Was heisst Denken* (GA 8), ed. Paola-Ludovika Coriando (Frankfurt am Main: Vittorio Klostermann, 2002), 149 ff.; *What is Called Thinking*, trans. Fred Wieck and J. Gray (New York: Harper & Row, 1968), 144 ff.

14 Emmanuel Levinas, "Paul Celan: From Being to Other," in *Proper Names*, trans. Michael Smith (Stanford, CA: Stanford University Press, 1996), 40–6.
15 GA 8: 161/130.
16 Nietzsche, "Schopenhauer as Educator," 137.

Chapter 1 The "Facticity of Life"

1 Hannah Arendt, *Briefe 1925 bis 1975 und andere Zeugnisse*, ed. Ursula Ludz (Frankfurt am Main: Vittorio Klostermann, 1998), 180; "Martin Heidegger at Eighty," trans. Albert Hofstadter (*The New York Review of Books*, October 21, 1971).
2 Martin Heidegger, *Ontologie (Hermeneutik der Faktizität)* (GA 63), ed. Kate Bröcker-Oltmanns (Frankfurt am Main: Vittorio Klostermann, 1988), 5; *Ontology: The Hermeneutics of Facticity*, trans. John van Buren (Bloomington, IN: Indiana University Press, 2009), 4.
3 [*Translator's note*: In the German academic system, a *Habilitationschrift* is something like a second PhD dissertation written for the purposes of being licensed to teach a designated subject at the university level.]
4 Martin Heidegger, *Anmerkungen I–V (Schwarze Hefte 1942–48)* (GA 97), ed. Peter Trawny (Frankfurt am Main: Vittorio Klostermann, 2015), 287 ff.; [*Translator's note*: An English translation by Adam Knowles is soon to appear with Indiana University Press.] For quite some time we have known that the text (*Grammatica speculativa*) Heidegger deals with in this work is not by Duns Scotus but rather by Thomas von Erfurt (date of birth and death unknown).
5 Martin Heidegger, *Grundprobleme der Phänomenologie (1919/20)* (GA 58), ed. Hans Helmuth Gander (Frankfurt am Main: Vittorio Klostermann, 1993), 35; *The Basic Problems of Phenomenology*, trans. Scott Campbell (New York: Bloomsbury, 2013), 29.
6 Martin Heidegger, *Phänomenologische Interpretationen zu Aristoteles. Einführung in die phänomenologische Forschung* (GA 61), ed. Walter Bröcker and Kate Bröcker-Oltmanns (Frankfurt am Main: Vittorio Klostermann, 1994), 89; *Phenomenological Interpretations of Aristotle. Initiation into Phenomenological Research*, trans. Richard Rojcewicz (Bloomington, IN: Indiana University Press, 2009), 67.
7 GA 58: 19/14. Italics added.
8 See Martin Heidegger, GA 1: 410 ff. and also *Zur Bestimmung der Philosophie* (GA 56/57), ed. Bernd Heimbüchel (Frankfurt am Main: Vittorio Klostermann, 1999), 64 sq; *Towards the Definition of Philosophy*, trans. Ted Sadler (London: Continuum, 2008), 124 ff.

9 GA 58: 33/27.

10 Ibid.

11 Ibid.: 22/17.

12 Martin Heidegger, *Phänomenologie des religiösen Lebens* (GA 60), ed. Matthias Jung, Thomas Regehly, and Claudius Strube (Frankfurt am Main: Vittorio Klostermann, 1995), 8; *Phenomenology of Religious Life*, trans. Matthias Fritsch and Jennifer Gosetti-Ferencei (Bloomington, IN: Indiana University Press, 2010), 7.

13 Ibid.: 8/6.

14 Ibid.: 8/7.

15 Ibid.

16 GA 56–7: 4/4.

17 [*Translator's note*: This is the first postwar course Heidegger gave at the University of Freiburg, entitled *Zur Bestimmung der Philosophie*. Its nickname *Kriegsnotsemester* has appropriately been translated into English as the "war-emergency-semester" by Theodore Kisiel. The course currently exists in published form in volumes 56–7 of Heidegger's *Gesamtausgabe*. Ted Sadler has produced an English translation of it entitled *Towards the Definition of Philosophy*, published by Continuum Press in 2008.]

18 GA 61: 70/52–3.

19 GA 58: 42/34.

20 GA 58: 105/83 [translation slightly modified].

21 GA 61: 187/141.

22 GA 63: 9/8.

23 GA 60: 63/43.

24 Martin Heidegger, *Phänomenologie der Anschauung und des Ausdrucks* (GA 59), ed. Claudius Strube (Frankfurt am Main: Vittorio Klostermann, 1993), 85; *Phenomenology of Intuition and Expression*, trans. Tracy Colony (London: Continuum, 2010), 65.

25 GA 61: 31/22.

26 Ibid.: 33/23 [translation slightly modified].

27 GA 95: 100/162.

28 GA 59: 35/25.

29 GA 61: 250/124.

30 GA 60: 135/96 [translation slightly modified].

31 GA 13: 113.

32 GA 12: 91/10.

33 GA 59: 91/72.

34 GA 60: 124/89.

35 No manuscript exists for the lecture course cited here: "Introduction to the Phenomenology of Religion" (winter semester, 1921). The *Gesamtausgabe* publication is based on notes.

36 GA 60: 80/57.

37 Ibid.: 69/48.

38 Ibid.: 95/66.
39 Ibid.: 121/87.
40 Ibid.: 119/85.
41 Ibid.: 98/66.
42 Ibid.: 104/73.
43 Ibid.: 114/81.
44 Ibid.: 110/78.
45 Ibid.: 155/110.
46 GA 9: 359/272.
47 GA 60: 68/48.
48 Donatella di Cesare, *Heidegger and the Jews: The Black Notebooks*, trans. Murtha Baca (Cambridge: Polity Press, 2018), 235 ff.
49 GA 60: 68/48.
50 Marlène Zarader, *La dette impensée: Heidegger et l'héritage hébraïque* (Paris: Editions du Seuil, 1999).
51 GA 5: 327/246–7.
52 GA 61: 61/46.
53 Ibid.: 85/64.
54 Ibid.: 60/45.
55 [*Translator's note*: I have consistently translated *Sein* as "being" throughout. For *Seiende*, the plural "beings" was used save for a few instances where an indefinite article ("*a* being") seemed better suited to capture the difference between *a* being – or particular beings – and being in general.]
56 Heidegger, *Phänomenologische Interpretationen zu Aristoteles: Ausarbeitung für die Marburger und Göttinger Philosophische Fakultät (1922)*, ed. Günther Neumann (Frankfurt am Main: Vittorio Klostermann, 2013), 42; "Phenomenological Interpretations in Connection with Aristotle: An Indication of the Hermeneutical Situation (1922)," in *Supplements: From the Earliest Essays to Being and Time and Beyond*, ed. John van Buren (Albany, NY: SUNY Press, 2002), 129.
57 Ibid.: 50/135.
58 Ibid.: 42, 55/129, 139.
59 Heidegger, *Platon: Sophistes* (GA 19), ed. Ingeborg Schüßler (Frankfurt am Main: Vittorio Klostermann, 1992), 11; *Plato's Sophist*, trans. Richard Rojcewicz and André Schuwer (Bloomington, IN: Indiana University Press, 2003), 8.
60 Ibid.: 245/169.
61 Ibid.: 257/177.
62 Plato, "Sophist," in *Theaetetus and Sophist*, ed. Christopher Rowe (Cambridge: Cambridge University Press, 2015), 140 [translation slightly modified].
63 GA 19: 447/309.
64 Ibid.: 466/323.

65 Ibid.

66 Ibid.: 467/323.

67 Hannah Arendt, "Martin Heidegger at Eighty," trans. Albert Hofstadter (*The New York Review of Books*, October 21, 1971).

68 Martin Heidegger, *Seminare* (GA 15), ed. Curd Ochwadt (Frankfurt am Main: Vittorio Klostermann, 2005), 437.

69 Sophie-Jan Arrien, *L'inquiétude de la pensée: L'herméneutique de la vie du jeune Heidegger (1919–1923)* (Paris: PUF, 2014).

Chapter 2 The "Meaning of Being"

1 Jürgen Habermas, "Heidegger – Werk und Weltanschauung," preface to the German edition of Victor Farías's book *Heidegger und der Nationalsozialismus*, trans. Klaus Laermann (Frankfurt am Main: S. Fischer, 1989), 13; an English translation of Habermas's preface has appeared in Habermas, *The New Conservatism: Cultural Criticism and the Historians' Debate*, trans. Shierry Nicholsen (Cambridge, MA: MIT Press, 1989), 153.

2 Emil Staiger, "Ein Rückblick," in *Heidegger heute: Perspektiven zur Deutung seines Werkes*, ed. Otto Pöggeler (Berlin: Athenäum Verlag, 1969), 242.

3 Heidegger, *Sein und Zeit* (GA 2), ed. Friedrich-Wilhelm von Herrmann (Frankfurt am Main: Vittorio Klostermann, 1978), 9; *Being and Time*, trans. Joan Stambaugh (Albany, NY: SUNY Press, 2010), 6.

4 GA 2: 316/228.

5 GA 65: 302.

6 Jacques Derrida has criticized the distinction that Heidegger almost always makes between humans and animals; see Derrida, "Geschlecht I: Sexual Difference, Ontological Difference," trans. Ruben Berezdivin and Elizabeth Rottenberg, in *Psyche: Inventions of the Other*, ed. Peggy Kamuf and Elizabeth Rottenberg (Stanford, CA: Stanford University Press, 2008), 27–62, and "Heidegger's Hand: Geschlecht II," trans. John P. Leavey Jr and Elizabeth Rottenberg, in *Psyche: Inventions of the Other* (Stanford, CA: Stanford University Press, 2008), 31 ff.

7 GA 2: 51/36.

8 Ibid.: 23/16.

9 Ibid.: 240/175.

10 Ibid.: 314/227 ff.

11 Ibid.: 24/17.

12 Ibid.: 577/415.

13 Ibid.: 152/111.

14 Heidegger, *Logik als die Frage nach dem Wesen der Sprache* (GA 38), ed. Günther Suebold (Frankfurt am Main: Vittorio Klostermann, 1998), 34; *Logic as the Question Concerning the Essence of Language*, trans. Wanda Gregory and Yvonne Unna (Albany, NY: SUNY Press, 2009), 31 [translation slightly modified].

15 GA 2: 152/111.

16 Ibid.: 166/121.

17 Ibid.: 162/118.

18 Ibid.: 256/186.

19 Ibid.: 168/121 ff.

20 Ibid.: 172/125.

21 Ibid.

22 *Martin Heidegger, Letters to his Wife (1915–1970)*, ed. Gertrud Heidegger, trans. R. Glasgow (Cambridge: Polity Press, 2010), 28.

23 GA 2: 245/178.

24 Ibid.: 247/179.

25 Ibid.: 248/180.

26 Ibid.

27 Ibid.: 248/181.

28 Ibid.

29 Peter Handke, *The Weight of the World*, trans. Ralph Manheim (New York: Farrar, Straus and Giroux, 1984).

30 GA 2: 249/181.

31 Ibid.: 249/181–2.

32 Jacques Lacan, *Anxiety: The Seminar of Jacques Lacan, Book X*, ed. Jacques Miller, trans. A. R. Price (Cambridge: Polity Press, 2015).

33 GA 2: 352/254.

34 GA 79: 17.

35 GA 2: 339/245 ff.

36 Ibid.: 350/253 ff.

37 Ibid.: 327/237 ff.

38 Max Scheler, *Späte Schriften*, ed. Manfred Frings (Munich: Francke Verlag, 1976), 294.

39 Ibid.: 297.

40 Emmanuel Levinas, *God, Death, and Time*, trans. Bettina Bergo (Stanford, CA: Stanford University Press, 2000), 12.

41 GA 2: 163/119.

42 Ibid.: 319/231.

43 Ibid.: 577/457.

44 Martin Heidegger, *Zum Ereignis Denken* (GA 73.2), ed. Peter Trawny (Frankfurt am Main: Vittorio Klostermann, 2013), 1275.

45 Heidegger, *Die Grundprobleme der Philosophie* (GA 24), ed. Friedrich-Wilhelm von Herrmann (Frankfurt am Main: Vittorio Klostermann, 1975), 322; *The Basic Problems of Phenomenology*, trans. Albert Hofstadter (Bloomington, IN: Indiana University Press, 1988), 227.

46 Ibid.: §6.

47 Ibid.: 402/284.

48 Ibid.: 404/285.

49 Paul Natorp, *Plato's Theory of Ideas: An Introduction to Idealism*, ed. Vasilis Politis (Sankt Augustin, Germany: Academia Verlag, 2004), 312.

50 See *Heidegger und der Neukantianismus (Studien und Materialien zum Neukantianismus)*, ed. Claudius Strube (Würzburg: Königshausen & Neumann, 2008).

51 Heidegger, *Einleitung in die Philosophie* (GA 27), ed. Otto Saame and Ina Saame-Speidel (Frankfurt am Main: Vittorio Klostermann, 1996), 394.

52 Ibid.: 425.

53 GA 9: 137/109.

54 This is not the only place where we could relate Heidegger's thinking to Plotinus. Why does Heidegger ignore Plotinus, given that he could have found in his work so many of the motifs of his own thinking? See Werner Beierwaltes, *Das wahre Selbst: Studien zu Plotins Begriff des Geistes und des Einen* (Frankfurt am Main: Vittorio Klostermann, 2001), 120 ff.

55 GA 9: 140/109–10.

56 Ibid.: 135/106.

57 GA 24: 15–16/11–12.

58 Ibid.: 460/323.

59 Ibid.: 27/20.

60 GA 9: 155/120.

61 GA 2: 14/12.

62 GA 63: 76/60.

63 GA 2: 47/33.

64 GA 19: 466/323.

65 GA 2: 514/370.

66 GA 7: 71; "Overcoming Metaphysics," in *The End of Philosophy*, trans. Joan Stambaugh (Chicago, IL: University of Chicago Press, 2003), 87.

67 GA 65: 250/197.

68 Ibid.

69 Ibid.: 425/336.

70 Ibid.: 465/366.

71 Ibid.: 116/92.

72 GA 9: 123/97.

73 Martin Heidegger, *Identität und Differenz* (GA 11), ed. Friedrich-Wilhelm von Herrmann (Frankfurt am Main: Vittorio Klostermann, 2006), 76; *Identity and Difference*, trans. Joan Stambaugh (Chicago, IL: University of Chicago Press, 2002), 70.

74 GA 73.2: 1330.

75 Ibid.: 1392.

76 Derrida, *Of Grammatology*, trans. Gayatri Spivak (Baltimore: Johns Hopkins University Press, 2016), 23.

77 Derrida, "Violence and Metaphysics," in *Writing and Difference*, trans. Alan Bass (Chicago, IL: University of Chicago Press, 1978), 137.

78 Ibid.: 90. Derrida's critique of Levinas is perhaps read with different eyes after the publication of *The Black Notebooks*.

79 For an exception to this rule, see Jean-Luc Nancy, "Heidegger's 'Originary Ethics,'" in *Heidegger and Practical Philosophy*, ed. François Raffoul and David Pettigrew (Albany, NY: SUNY Press, 2002), 65–86.

80 GA 60: 31/22.

81 GA 2: 27/19.

82 Ibid.: 507/365.

83 Ibid.: 509/366.

84 Ibid.: 3/1.

85 Ibid.: 510/367.

86 Ibid.: 507/365.

87 Ibid.: 508/366.

88 Ibid.: 518/373.

89 Heidegger, *Besinnung* (GA 66), ed. Friedrich-Wilhelm von Herrmann (Frankfurt am Main: Vittorio Klostermann, 1997), 169; *Mindfulness*, trans. Parvis Emad and Thomas Kalary (London: Bloomsbury Academic, 2006), 147.

90 GA 2: 28/20.

91 GA 65: 492/387.

92 Heidegger, *Die Geschichte des Seyns* (GA 69), ed. Peter Trawny (Frankfurt am Main: Vittorio Klostermann, 1998), 170; *The History of Beyng*, trans. Jeffrey Powell and Will McNeill (Bloomington, IN: Indiana University Press, 2015), 145.

93 GA 9: 138/108.

94 See Dieter Thomä, *Die Zeit des Selbst und die Zeit danach: Zur Kritik der Textgeschichte Martin Heideggers 1910–1976* (Frankfurt am Main: Suhrkamp Verlag, 1990).

95 GA 97: 98.

96 GA 95: 408/318.

97 Karl Löwith, *My Life in Germany Before and After 1933*, trans. Elizabeth King (Chicago, IL: University of Illinois Press, 1994), 60.

Chapter 3 The "History of Being"

1 Heidegger, *Leitgedanken zur Entstehung der Metaphysik, der neuzeitlichen Wissenschaft und der modernen Technik* (GA 76), ed. Claudius Strube (Frankfurt am Main: Vittorio Klostermann, 2009), 233; Andrew Mitchell and Christopher Merwin are preparing a translation of this volume for Indiana University Press.

2 Heidegger, *Überlegungen II–VI (Schwarze Hefte: 1931–1938)* (GA 94), ed. Peter Trawny (Frankfurt am Main: Vittorio Klostermann, 2014), 111; *Ponderings II–VI: The Black Notebooks 1931–1938*, trans. Richard Rojcewicz (Bloomington, IN: Indiana University Press, 2016), 81.

3 GA 2: 28/20.

4 GA 73.2: 1277.

5 Heidegger, *Sein und Wahrheit* (GA 36/37), ed. Hartmut Tietjen (Frankfurt am Main: Vittorio Klostermann, 2001), 115; *Being and Truth*, trans. Gregory Fried and Richard Polt (Bloomington, IN: Indiana University Press, 2001), 91.

6 Ibid.: 116/91.

7 In *Being and Time*, Heidegger refers to the "sole authority that a free existence can have for the possibilities of existence that can be repeated," that is to say, for the "heritage" of "history" (GA 2: 516/372). In *Contributions to Philosophy*, he clarifies that "speaking is not something over and against what is to be said but is this latter itself as the essential occurrence of beyng" (GA 65: 4/6). In this sense, the author of the "history of being" is this very history itself.

8 GA 35: 1/1.

9 Ibid.: 42/33.

10 Ibid.: 47, 99/36, 75 [translation modified].

11 Ibid.: 98–9/74–5.

12 Ibid.: 1/1.

13 GA 94: 26, 107/20, 79.

14 Ibid.: 111/81.

15 Ibid.: 39/30. For revolution in Heidegger, see Florian Grosser, *Revolution denken: Heidegger und das Politische 1919–1969* (Munich, C. H. Beck, 2011).

16 GA 97: 19.

17 GA 69: 23/22.

18 GA 94: 110/81.

19 Heidegger, "Die Selbstbehauptung der deutschen Universität," in *Reden und andere Zeugnisse eines Lebenweges* (GA 16), ed. Hermann Heidegger (Frankfurt am Main: Vittorio Klostermann, 2000), 107; "The Self-Assertion of the German University," trans.

William Lewis, in *The Heidegger Controversy,* ed. Richard Wolin (Cambridge, MA: MIT Press, 1993), 29.

20 Ibid.: 114/36 [translation slightly modified].

21 It is worth comparing this articulation of the State with Plato's division of society into classes in the *Republic.* In a mythological language, Plato aligns gold, silver, and bronze with rulers, guardians, and farmers respectively (415 a). To put it crudely, there is a parallel to Heidegger's project given that the latter no doubt considers the knowers to be rulers.

22 GA 95: title page of *Ponderings VII.*

23 GA 94: 118/87.

24 Ibid.: 135, 142/99, 104.

25 Ibid.: 162/119.

26 Ibid.: 194/142.

27 GA 95: 18/14.

28 Heidegger, *Überlegungen XII–XV (Schwarze Hefte 1931–38)* (GA 96), ed. Peter Trawny (Frankfurt am Main: Vittorio Klostermann, 2014), 127; *Ponderings XII–XV, Black Notebooks*, trans. Richard Rojcewicz (Bloomington, IN: Indiana University Press, 2017), 99.

29 GA 95: 408/318.

30 GA 96: 131/103.

31 Ibid.: 132/103.

32 Ibid.: 133/103–4.

33 Ibid.: 141/110.

34 Ibid.: 142/100.

35 GA 97: 70.

36 See Norbert von Hellingrath, *Hölderlin: Zwei Vorträge, Hölderlin und die Deutschen, Hölderlins Wahnsinn* (Munich: Hugo Bruckmann Verlag, 1921).

37 Heidegger, *Hölderlins Hymnen "Germanien" und "Der Rhein"* (GA 39), ed. Susanne Ziegler (Frankfurt am Main: Vittorio Klostermann, 1984), 9; *Hölderlin's Hymns "Germania" and "The Rhine,"* trans. Will McNeill and Julia Ireland (Bloomington, IN: Indiana University Press, 2014), 9.

38 Heidegger, *Zu Hölderlin – Griechenlandreisen* (GA 75), ed. Curd Ochwadt (Frankfurt am Main: Vittorio Klostermann, 2000), 161.

39 Ibid.: 82.

40 GA 36/37: 103/82.

41 Ibid.: 104/83.

42 GA 38: 170/146.

43 The text published as volume 38 of the *Gesamtausgabe* is a transcript. Heidegger's manuscript has surfaced in the meantime and will be edited in the coming years.

44 See GA 12: 151/60.

45 Heidegger, *Erläuterungen zur Hölderlins Dichtung* (GA 4), ed. Friedrich-Wilhelm von Herrmann (Frankfurt am Main: Vittorio Klostermann, 1977), 35; *Elucidations of Hölderlin's Poetry*, trans. Keith Hoeller (Amherst, NY: Humanity Books, 2000), 53.

46 GA 38: 168/144 [translation slightly modified].

47 GA 4: 41/59.

48 Ibid.: 43/60.

49 Ibid.: 34/52.

50 Ibid.: 43/60.

51 GA 16: 333.

52 GA 39: 220/201.

53 GA 94: 27/21.

54 GA 39: 214/195.

55 Carl Schmitt, *The Concept of the Political*, trans. George Schwab (Chicago, IL: University of Chicago Press, 2007).

56 GA 39: 288/261.

57 Friedrich Hölderlin, *Essays and Letters on Theory*, ed. and trans. Thomas Pfau (Albany, NY: SUNY Press, 1988), 150.

58 GA 39: 293/266.

59 Heidegger, *Über den Anfang* (GA 70), ed. Paola-Ludovika Coriando (Frankfurt am Main: Vittorio Klostermann, 2005), 149.

60 GA 39: 55/53.

61 GA 97: 70.

62 GA 70: 167.

63 GA 39: 38/38.

64 Heidegger, *Hölderlins Hymne "Der Ister,"* ed. Walter Biemel (Frankfurt am Main: Vittorio Klostermann, 1984), 63; *Hölderlin's Hymn "The Ister,"* trans. Will McNeill and Julia David (Bloomington, IN: Indiana University Press, 1996), 51.

65 For an example, see Jochen Schmidt, "Hölderlin im 20. Jahrhundert: Rezeption und Edition," in *Hölderlin und die Moderne: eine Bestandsaufnahme*, ed. Gerhard Kurz, Valérie Lawitschka, and Jürgen Wertheimer (Tübingen: Attempto, 1995), 105–25. For an influential exception to this rule, see Beda Allemann, *Hölderlin and Heidegger* (Zürich: Atlantis Verlag, 1954).

66 Max Kommerell, *Briefe und Aufzeichnungen 1919–1944*, ed. Inge Jens (Olten: Walter-Verlag, 1967), 397.

67 *Martin Heidegger, Letters to his Wife (1915–1970)*, ed. Gertrud Heidegger, trans. R. Glasgow (Cambridge: Polity Press, 2010), 28. At the end of the nineteenth century, the concept of "Jewification" already belongs to the anti-Semitic lexicon. See Walther Rathenau, "Höre Israel," in *19. Jahrhunderts zum antisemitischen Wortschatz: Ein Disput unter Juden aus Deutschland*, ed. Christoph Schulte

(Stuttgart: Reclam Verlag, 1993), 37; "The goal to oppose the Jewification (*Verjudung*) of life in the public sphere is legitimate." Rathenau's essay, published under a pseudonym in 1897, would require a longer interpretation.

68 *Martin Heidegger, Letters to his Wife (1915–1970)*, 77.

69 Karl Jaspers, *Philosophische Autobiographie* (Munich: Piper-Verlag, 1977), 101.

70 *Die Protokolle der Weisen von Zion: Die Grundlage des modernen Antisemitismus – eine Fälschung*, ed. Jeffrey Sammons (Göttingen: Wallstein Verlag, 1998). Cf. also on the protocols, Wolfgang Benz, *Die Protokolle der Weisen von Zion: Die Legende von der jüdischen Weltverschwörung* (Munich: C. H. Beck, 2011).

71 Alexander Stein, *Adolf Hitler "Schüler der Weisen von Zion"* (Karlsbad: Verlagsanstalt Graphia, 1936).

72 Hannah Arendt, *The Origins of Totalitarianism* (New York: Harcourt, 1994), 358.

73 Ibid.: 378.

74 *Martin Heidegger, Letters to his Wife (1915–1970)*, 80.

75 *Letters 1925–1975, Hannah Arendt and Martin Heidegger*, trans. Andrew Shields (New York: Harcourt, 2004), 52–3.

76 GA 96: 118/93.

77 Ibid.: 56/44.

78 Heidegger is presumably thinking of matrilineal descent in Judaism, according to which Jewish descent is traced through the maternal line.

79 Cf. GA 94: 189/139.

80 GA 96: 243/191.

81 GA 97: 20.

82 Hitler speaks of the "destructive principle of the Jews." See Hitler, *Mein Kampf*, trans. Alvin Johnson (New York: Reynal and Hitchcock, 1940), 666. Mommsen coins the influential formulation that Jewry is "the actual ferment of cosmopolitanism and national decomposition." See Theodor Mommsen, *History of Rome, Vol. 4*, trans. William Dickson (New York: Charles Scribner, 1871), 643.

83 GA 97: 20.

84 Emmanuel Levinas, "As if Consenting to Horror," trans. Paula Wissing, in *Critical Inquiry, Special Feature on Heidegger and Nazism* 15(2) (1989): 488.

85 GA 97: 159; this passage has been translated by Andrew Mitchell in Peter Trawny, *The Myth of World Jewish Conspiracy*, 88.

86 See *The Complete Hitler. A Digital Desktop Reference to his Speeches and Proclamations*, ed. Max Domarus, trans. Mary Golbert (Wauconda, IL: Bolchazy-Carducci Publishers, 2007). Here we read: "I have been a prophet very often in my lifetime, and this

earned me mostly ridicule. In the time of my struggle for power, it was primarily the Jewish people who mocked my prophecy that, one day, I would assume leadership of this Germany, of this State, and of the entire Volk, and that I would press for a resolution of the Jewish question, among many other problems. The resounding laughter of the Jews in Germany then may well be stuck in their throats today, I suspect. Once again I will be a prophet: should the international Jewry of finance succeed, both within and beyond Europe, in plunging mankind into yet another world war, then the result will not be a Bolshevization of the earth and the victory of Jewry, but the annihilation of the Jewish race in Europe" (1449).

87 Emmanuel Faye, *Heidegger: The Introduction of National Socialism into Philosophy in Light of the Unpublished Seminars of 1933–1935*, trans. Michael Smith (New Haven, CT: Yale University Press, 2011).

88 See Paul Ricoeur, *Freud & Philosophy: An Essay on Interpretation*, trans. Denis Savage (New Haven, CT: Yale University Press, 1970), 32 ff. Here, the context of the hermeneutics of "suspicion" is psychoanalysis. Nietzsche and Marx are also among the "masters of suspicion."

89 GA 65: 349/276 [translation modified].

90 Leo Strauss, *Natural Right and History* (Chicago, IL: University of Chicago Press, 1950). "The final and irrevocable insight into the historical character of all thought would transcend history only if that insight were accessible to man as man, and hence, in principle, at all times; but it does not transcend history if it essentially belongs to a specific historical situation. It belongs to a specific historical situation: that situation is not merely the condition of the historicist's insight but its source" (28). No one has understood Heidegger's relationship to "history" as clearly as Strauss. Heidegger's "insight" into the "history of being" is itself a "destiny," that is to say, it belongs to the narrative understanding that Heidegger must give himself. Only a "German" can be blessed with *this* insight precisely in *this* place and at *this* time (28).

91 GA 65: 429/339.

92 Ibid.: 7–8/9.

93 Ibid.: 436/344.

94 Ibid.: 423/334.

95 Ibid.: 6/8.

96 Ibid.: 438/275.

97 GA 2: 177/129.

98 GA 65: 352/278.

99 Ibid.: 93/74.

100 Ibid.: 98/78.

101 Ibid.: 11/11.

102 Ibid.: 113/89.

103 Ibid.

104 Ibid.: 247/194.

105 Ibid.: 310/245.

106 For a phenomenology of "responsiveness," see Bernhard Waldenfels, *Antwortregister* (Frankfurt am Main: Suhrkamp Verlag, 1994). The "responsive" fundamental structure of Heidegger's thought must be thought together with the "mytho-logy of the event of appropriation." As it understands itself, the narrativity of Heideggerian philosophy is "responsive." Ultimately what is narrated is the "voice of being," which does not announce itself in clear and distinct concepts (GA 54: 250/167).

107 Heidegger, *Seminare Hegel – Schelling* (GA 86), ed. Peter Trawny (Frankfurt am Main: Vittorio Klostermann, 2011), 471.

108 GA 65: 349/276 [translation modified].

109 Ibid.: 407/323.

110 Ibid.

111 Ibid.: 251/198.

112 Cf. GA 65: 238/188.

113 Ibid.: 4/6.

114 Heidegger, *Der Ursprung des Kunstwerkes*, ed. Friedrich-Wilhelm von Herrmann (Frankfurt am Main: Vittorio Klostermann, 2012); "The Origin of the Work of Art," in *Off the Beaten Track*, trans. and ed. Julian Young and Kenneth Haynes (Cambridge: Cambridge University Press, 2002), 50.

115 Ibid.: 65/49; GA 65: 389/307.

116 Heidegger, "Die Kunst und der Raum," in *Aus der Erfahrung des Denkens 1910–1976* (GA 13), ed. Hermann Heidegger (Frankfurt am Main: Vittorio Klostermann, 1983), 208; *Art and Space*, trans. Charles Seibert (The Hague: Nijhoff, 1970), 7. On the relation between "sculpture" and "place," see Andrew Mitchell's quite beautiful book *Heidegger Among the Sculptors: Body, Space, and the Art of Dwelling* (Stanford, CA: Stanford University Press, 2010).

117 Heidegger, "The Origin of the Work of Art," 13.

118 Ibid.: 27.

119 GA 2: 21/15–16.

120 Ibid.: 86/63.

121 Ibid.: 89/66.

122 Ibid.: 90, 92/67, 68.

123 Ibid.: 112/82.

124 Ibid.: 114/84.

125 Ibid.: 115/85.

126 Hubert L. Dreyfus's interpretation of Heidegger relates almost exclusively to Heidegger's analysis of "useful things." See: Hubert Dreyfus, *What Computers Still Can't Do* (London: MIT Press, 1992).

127 GA 39: 88/80.

128 Heidegger, "The Origin of the Work of Art," 31 [translation slightly modified].

129 GA 36/37: 89/72 ff.

130 Heidegger, "The Origin of the Work of Art," 26.

131 This sentence originally appears in a prose text, though the Hölderlin edition by Nobert von Hellingrath that Heidegger always uses provides a line break. See Friedrich Hölderlin, *Sämtliche Werke und Briefe*, ed. Michael Knaupp (Munich: Carl Hanser Verlag, 1992), 908.

132 See Martin Heidegger, "... dichterisch wohnet der Mensch ...," in GA 7: 189–209; "... Poetically, Man Dwells ...," trans. Albert Hofstadter, in Martin Heidegger, *Philosophical and Political Writings*, ed. Manfred Stassen (New York: Continuum International Publishing, 2003), 265–79.

133 GA 39: 105/95.

134 Emmanuel Levinas, "Heidegger, Gagarin and Us," in *Difficult Freedom: Essays on Judaism*, trans. Sean Hand (London: Athlone Press, 1990), 231–4.

135 GA 65: 29/25.

136 Ibid.: 69/55.

137 Ibid.: 277/218 ff.

138 GA 95: 51/39.

139 Ibid.: 503/396.

140 Ibid.: 505/397.

141 Jürgen Habermas, *Postmetaphysical Thinking*, trans. William Hohengarten (Cambridge, MA: MIT Press, 1993), 29.

142 GA 2: 27/19.

143 Ibid.: 30/21.

144 Ibid.: 31/22.

145 GA 38: 11/9.

146 Heidegger, *Einführung in die Metaphysik* (GA 40), ed. Peter Jaeger (Frankfurt am Main: Vittorio Klostermann, 1983), 197; *Introduction to Metaphysics*, trans. Richard Polt and Gregory Fried (New Haven, CT: Yale University Press, 2014), 210.

147 GA 38: 1/1.

148 GA 40: 129/134.

149 GA 38: 10/3.

150 See Immanuel Kant, *Groundwork of the Metaphysics of Morals*, trans. and ed. Mary Gregor and Jens Timmermann (Cambridge: Cambridge University Press, 2012).

151 Heidegger, *Heraklit* (GA 55), ed. Manfred Frings (Frankfurt am Main: Vittorio Klostermann, 1994), 186 ff.

152 Heidegger, *Die Grundbegriffe der Metaphysik: Welt, Endlichkeit, Einsamkeit*, ed. Friedrich-Wilhelm von Herrmann (Frankfurt am Main: Vittorio Klostermann, 1983), 438; *The Fundamental Concepts of Metaphysics*, trans. Will McNeill and Nicholas Walker (Bloomington, IN: Indiana University Press, 1995), 302.

153 GA 55: 196.

154 Hegel, *Lectures on the Philosophy of World History*, trans. H. B. Nisbet (Cambridge: Cambridge University Press, 1975), 89.

155 Hegel, *Elements of the Philosophy of Right*, ed. Allen Wood, trans. H. B. Nisbet (Cambridge: Cambridge University Press, 1991), 20.

156 GA 7: 218; "Logos: Heraclitus (Fragment B 50)," in *Early Greek Thinking*, trans. David Krell and Frank Capuzzi (New York: Harper Collins, 1975), 64.

157 One important step in this respect is the uncoupling of truth and the statement, the determination of truth as "unconcealment," which appears for the first time in the lecture on the "Essence of Truth" from 1930 (GA 9: 177–202). See also my book *Freedom to Fail: Heidegger's Anarchy*, trans. Ian Moore and Christopher Turner (Cambridge: Polity Press, 2015).

158 GA 94: 27/21.

159 GA 7: 81; "Overcoming Metaphysics," in *The End of Philosophy*, trans. Joan Stambaugh (Chicago, IL: University of Chicago Press, 2003), 95.

160 Ibid.: 93/106.

161 GA 65: 423/335.

162 GA 66: 128/108.

163 GA 7: 69/85.

164 Ibid.: 77/91 [translation modified].

165 GA 65: 430/339–40.

166 GA 2: 213/155.

167 Ibid.: 214/156.

168 The problem no doubt stems from the fact that Heidegger presupposes in fact an understanding of the word as object. In this sense, we should not see in his comment on "words as things" a mere rhetorical effect.

169 GA 2: 220/160.

170 GA 36/37, 103/82.

171 Ibid.: 104/83.

172 GA 38: 170/146.

173 Ibid.: 11/9.

174 GA 65: 78/62.

175 Ibid.: 11/11.

176 Heidegger, *Zur Sache des Denkens* (GA 14), ed. Friedrich-Wilhelm von Herrmann (Frankfurt am Main: Vittorio Klostermann, 2007), 30; *On Time and Being*, trans. Joan Stambaugh (Chicago, IL: Chicago University Press, 2002), 24.

177 Ibid.: 6/2.

178 GA 65: 78/62.

179 GA 12: 30; "Language," in *Language, Poetry, Thought*, trans. Albert Hoftstadter (New York: Harper & Row, 1975), 210.

180 Here too a comparison with certain of Wittgenstein's ideas could be productive. On the question of language in Heidegger and Wittgenstein, see Matthias Flatscher, *Logos und Lethe: Zur Phänomenologischen Sprachauffassung im Spätwerk von Heidegger und Wittgenstein* (Freiburg and Munich: K. Alber, 2011).

181 GA 75: 201.

182 GA 12: 27/207.

183 [*Translator's note*: As Trawny himself notes later on: "In German, the prefix *Ge-* characterizes a gathering of different elements that belong together. For example, a *Gebirge* (mountain range) is the gathering of different *Berge* (mountains)."]

184 Norbert Wiener, *Cybernetics, or Control and Communication in the Animal and the Machine* (New York: J. Wiley, 1952).

185 GA 9: 313/239.

186 GA 16: 671; "Only a God can save us" (*Der Spiegel*'s interview), trans. Maria Alter and John Caputo, in *The Heidegger Controversy*, 91–118.

187 GA 66: 415/368.

188 GA 9: 61/50.

189 GA 16: 111; "The Self-Assertion of the German University," in *The Heidegger Controversy*, 33.

190 Nietzsche, *The Gay Science*, ed. Bernard Williams, trans. Josephine Nauckhoff (Cambridge: Cambridge University Press, 2001), 119.

191 Cf. GA 94: 463/336.

192 GA 5: 216/162.

193 GA 4: 194/224.

194 GA 75: 51.

195 GA 39: 147/128.

196 Cf. Christian Sommer, "Heidegger, politische Theologie," in *Heidegger, die Juden, noch einmal*, ed. Peter Trawny and Andrew Mitchell (Frankfurt am Main: Vittorio Klostermann, 2015), 43–53. Heidegger scholarship owes much to Christian Sommer and his research on Heidegger's situation around 1933. See too Christian Sommer, *Heidegger 1933: Le programme platonicien du Discours de rectorat* (Paris: Hermann, 2013).

197 GA 39: 220/201.

198 GA 65: 437/345.
199 Ibid.: 248/195.
200 Ibid.: 403/319.
201 Ibid.: 405/321.
202 GA 5: 327/246.
203 GA 16: 671/107.
204 GA 97: 199.
205 Ibid.: 205.
206 Ibid.: 369.
207 Ibid.: 438.

Chapter 4 The "Essence of Technology"

1 Rüdiger Safranski, *Martin Heidegger: Between Good and Evil*, trans. Ewald Osers (Cambridge, MA: Harvard University Press, 1998), 393.
2 GA 16: 375; "The Rectorate 1933/34 – Facts and Thoughts," trans. Karsten Harries, *The Review of Metaphysics* 38(3) (March 1985): 481–502.
3 GA 2: 169/123.
4 Ernst Jünger, *Copse 125: A Chronicle from the Trench Warfare of 1918*, trans. Basil Creighton (New York: Howard Fertig, 2003).
5 Ernst Jünger, *The Worker: Dominion and Form*, ed. Laurence Hemming, trans. Bogdan Costea and Laurence Hemming (Evanston, IL: Northwestern University Press, 2017), 97.
6 Friedrich Nietzsche, *The Will to Power*, trans. Walter Kaufmann and R. J. Hollingdale (New York: Vintage Books, 1968), 399.
7 Friedrich Nietzsche, *Human, All Too Human: A Book for Free Spirits*, trans. R. J. Hollingdale (Cambridge: Cambridge University Press, 1986), 366.
8 Ernst Jünger, "Total Mobilization," in *The Heidegger Controversy: A Critical Reader*, ed. Richard Wolin (Cambridge, MA: MIT Press, 1993), 134.
9 Ibid.: 139.
10 GA 16: 205.
11 Ibid.: 204.
12 Ibid.: 206.
13 GA 94: 356/260.
14 Heidegger, *Zu Ernst Jünger* (GA 90), ed. Peter Trawny (Frankfurt am Main: Vittorio Klostermann, 2004), 33.
15 GA 96: 224/176.
16 GA 97: 171.
17 GA 90: 29.

18 GA 40: 112/163.
19 GA 13: 36.
20 GA 5: 87/66.
21 GA 69: 186/158.
22 Ibid.: 46/41.
23 GA 69: 186/158.
24 GA 94: 364/265.
25 GA 69: 23/22.
26 Ibid.: 24/22.
27 GA 69: 47/42.
28 GA 97: 18.
29 Ibid.: 20.
30 GA 73.1: 843.
31 GA 79: 26/25.
32 Ibid.: 27/26.
33 Ibid.: 27/27.
34 Arendt, *Origins of Totalitarianism*, X.
35 GA 97: 20.
36 GA 79: 31/30.
37 Ibid.: 32/31.
38 Ibid.: 33/31.
39 Ibid.: 60/56.
40 GA 76: 258.
41 Ibid.: 325.
42 The most detailed, rigorous, and successful analysis of the thinking of the "fourfold" is Andrew Mitchell's work *The Fourfold: Reading the Late Heidegger* (Evanston, IL: Northwestern University Press, 2015).
43 GA 79: 6/5.
44 Ibid.: 12/11.
45 Ibid.: 13/12.
46 Ibid.: 6/5.
47 GA 198: 65/155.
48 GA 79: 25/24.
49 Ibid.: 46/44.
50 Ibid.: 21/20.
51 Ibid.: 20/19.
52 GA 27: 394.
53 "The Origin of the Work of Art," 23.
54 Ibid.
55 Ibid.
56 GA 60: 69/48.
57 Cf. Christian Sommer, "Heidegger, politische Theologie," in *Heidegger, die Juden, noch einmal*, ed. Peter Trawny and Andrew Mitchell (Frankfurt am Main: Vittorio Klostermann, 2015), 43–53.

Heidegger scholarship owes much to Christian Sommer and his research on Heidegger's situation around 1933. See too Christian Sommer, *Heidegger 1933: Le programme platonicien du Discours de rectorat* (Paris: Hermann, 2013).

58 GA 95: 97/76.

59 GA 96: 56/44.

60 GA 79: 17/16.

61 Ibid.

62 Ibid.: 18/18.

63 Ibid.: 17/16.

64 Ibid.

65 Ibid.: 56/53.

66 Ibid.: 56/54.

67 Elie Wiesel, "The Death of My Father," in *Legends of Our Time* (New York: Schocken, 1968), 2. Elie Wiesel's father died in Buchenwald, thus not an extermination camp, to return to the different functions of the camps. Arendt and Adorno share Heidegger's interpretation according to which death "in masses" is not a death carried out by the deceased. I would like to ask here: death has an aspect that is like a complete obverse with respect to the objective circumstances of the situation in which it takes place. How can one deny those who died in the gas chambers the ability to have died in possession of their death? Does this not give the executioner a final victory to acknowledge that he could "take possession" of the death he gives? Naturally, what distinguishes Elie Wiesel from Heidegger, Arendt, and Adorno is that he was a witness.

68 GA 97: 56/54.

69 GA 79: 21/20.

70 GA 76: 233.

71 GA 14: 63/53.

Chapter 5 Reverberations

1 Dominique Janicaud, *Heidegger in France*, trans. François Raffoul and David Pettygrew (Bloomington, IN: Indiana University Press, 2015). In France, names such as Jean-Luc Nancy, Jean-Luc Marion, and also Alain Badiou – who has recently published his seminars on Heidegger (*Heidegger: L'être III – Figure du retrait, 1986–1987*, Paris: Fayard, 2015) – inform the current debate.

2 Rudolf Carnap, "The Overcoming of Metaphysics through the Logical Analysis of Language," in *Heidegger and Modern Philosophy: Critical Essays*, ed. Michale Murray (New Haven, CT: Yale University Press, 1978).

3 Hans-Georg Gadamer, *Truth and Method*, trans. Joel Weinsheimer and Donald G. Marshall (London: Continuum, 2004), 172–382.

4 Derrida, *Of Grammatology*, 11 ff.

5 Emmanuel Levinas, "Bewunderung und Enttäuschung," in *Antwort: Martin Heidegger im Gespräch*, ed. Günther Neske and Emil Kettering (Pfüllingen: Neske, 1988), 163 ff.

6 See Emmanuel Levinas, "Heidegger, Gagarin and Us."

7 Hannah Arendt, *The Human Condition* (Chicago, IL: University of Chicago Press, 1998).

8 Arendt's explanation of the "banality of evil" is founded on the absence of reflection by Eichmann: see Hannah Arendt, *Eichmann in Jerusalem: A Report on the Banality of Evil* (London: Penguin Classics, 2006), 288: "That such remoteness from reality and thoughtlessness can wreak more havoc than all the evil instincts taken together which, perhaps, are inherent in man – that was, in fact, the lesson one could learn in Jerusalem." Heidegger discusses the absence of reflection in detail in the course "What is Called Thinking?," published in 1954.

9 Theodor Adorno, *The Jargon of Authenticity*, trans. Knut Tarnowski and Frederic Will (Evanston, IL: Northwestern University Press, 1973), 5–6.

10 Ibid.: 160.

11 Ibid.: 5–6.

12 Günther Anders, *Über Heidegger*, ed. G. Oberschlick (Munich: Beck, 2001), 61 ff. and 278 ff.

13 Georg Lukács, *The Destruction of Reason*, trans. Peter Palmer (London: Merlin, 1980), 509.

14 Ibid.

15 Ibid.: 500.

16 Peter Sloterdijk, *Not Saved: Essays After Heidegger*, trans. Ian Alexander Moore and Christopher Turner (Cambridge: Polity Press, 2017), xi.

17 GA 86: 471.

18 Jean-Luc Nancy, "Heidegger's 'Originary Ethics,'" trans. Duncan Large, in *Heidegger and Practical Philosophy*, ed. François Raffoul and David Pettigrew (Albany, NY: SUNY Press, 2002), 65–86.

19 Ibid.: 65.

20 Ibid.: 71.

21 Ibid.: 80.

22 See *Kittler Now: Current Perspectives in Kittler Studies*, ed. Stephen Sale and Laura Salisbury (Cambridge: Polity Press, 2015).

23 Gerhart Baumann, *Erinnerungen an Paul Celan* (Frankfurt am Main: Suhrkamp, 1992), 59 ff.

24 Alain Badiou, *Manifesto for Philosophy*, trans. and ed. Norman Madarasz (Albany, NY: SUNY Press, 1999), 86.

25 Quoted in James K. Lyon, *Paul Celan and Martin Heidegger: An Unresolved Conversation, 1951–1970* (Baltimore, MD: Johns Hopkins University Press, 2006), 207.

26 Botho Strauß, *Der Aufstand gegen der sekundären Welt: Bemerkungen zu einer Aesthetik der Anwesenheit* (Munich: Hanser Verlag, 1999), 66.

27 Botho Strauß, "Heideggers Gedichte. Eine Feuerprobe unserer kommunikativen Intelligenz: Zum einhundertachtzigsten Band der Gasamtausgabe," in *Heidegger und die Literatur*, ed. G. Figal and U. Faulff (Frankfurt am Main: Vittorio Klostermann, 2012), 15.

28 Peter Handke, *Aber ich lebe von den Zwischenräumen. Ein Gespräch geführt von Herbert Gamper* (Zürich: Amman Verlag, 1987), 206.

29 Peter Handke, *Abschied des Träumers vom Neunten Land. Eine Wirklichkeit, die vergangen ist: Erinnerungen an Slowenien* (Frankfurt am Main: Suhrkamp, 1991), 13 ff.

30 Victor Farías, *Heidegger and Nazism*, trans. Paul Burrell and Gabriel Ricci, ed. Joseph Margolis and Tom Rockmore (Philadelphia, PA: Temple University Press, 1989). Farías's position is weakened by confusions of the following type: Heidegger's quotation of a sermon by Abraham a Sancta Clara, from the seventeenth century ("Our peace is as far removed from the war as Sachsenhausen from Frankfurt") is related by Farías to the concentration camp near Berlin, whereas it is in fact referring to a neighborhood in Frankfurt.

31 Faye, *Heidegger: The Introduction of National Socialism into Philosophy*, xxv.

32 Ibid.: 195.

33 Holger Zaborowski, *Eine Frage von Irre und Schuld?* (Frankfurt am Main: Fischer, 2010).

34 See Donatella di Cesare, *Heidegger and the Jews*. In my book *Heidegger and the Myth of a Jewish World Conspiracy*, I myself refer to a "being-historical anti-Semitism." In doing so, however, I am not at all attempting a "sublimation" of Heidegger's anti-Semitism (as Jürgen Habermas suggests in an interview given in the journal *Esprit* 8, 2015). It is impossible to "sublimate" anti-Semitism; it is a matter, on the contrary, of "desublimating" the history of being.

Biographical Facts in Historical Context

1 GA 58: 30/25 [translation slightly modified].

Bibliography

Arrien, Sophie-Jan, 2014, *L'inquiétude de la pensée: L'herméneutique de la vie du jeune Heidegger (1919–1923)*. Paris: PUF.

Badiou, Alain, 2015, *Heidegger: L'être III – Figure du retrait, 1986–1987*. Paris: Fayard.

Denker, Alfred, 2011, *Unterwegs in Sein und Zeit: Einführung in Leben und Denken von Martin Heidegger*. Stuttgart: Klett-Cota.

Denker, Alfred and Zaborowski, Holger (eds), 2004, *Heidegger-Jahrbuch*. Freiburg: Karl Alber Verlag.

Derrida, Jacques, 1978, *Writing and Difference*, trans. Alan Bass. Chicago, IL: University of Chicago Press.

Di Cesare, Donatella, 2018, *Heidegger and the Jews: The Black Notebooks*, trans. Murtha Baca. Cambridge: Polity Press.

Dieter, Thomä (ed.) 2013, *Heidegger-Handbuch: Leben – Werk – Wirkung*. Stuttgart: J. B. Metzler.

Faye, Emmanuel, 2011, *Heidegger: The Introduction of National Socialism into Philosophy in Light of the Unpublished Seminars of 1933–1935*, trans. Michael Smith. New Haven, CT: Yale University Press.

Heidegger, Gertrud (ed.), 2010, *Martin Heidegger, Letters to his Wife (1915–1970)*, trans. R. Glasgow. Cambridge: Polity Press.

Heidegger, Martin, 2008, *Eine gefährliche Irrnis*, in *Jahresgabe der Martin-Heidegger Gesellschaft* 2008.

Hölderlin, Friedrich, 1992, *Sämtliche Werke und Briefe*, ed. Michael Knaupp. Munich: Carl Hanser Verlag.

Janicaud, Dominique, 2015, *Heidegger in France*, trans. François Raffoul and David Pettygrew. Bloomington, IN: Indiana University Press.

Levinas, Emmanuel, 2000, *God, Death and Time*, trans. Bettina Bergo. Stanford, CA: Stanford University Press.

Mehring, Reinhard, 1992, *Heideggers Überlieferungsgeschick: eine dionysische Inszenierung*. Würzburg: Königshausen & Neumann.

Mitchell, Andrew, 2015, *The Fourfold: Reading the Late Heidegger*. Evanston, IL: Northwestern University Press.

Nancy, Jean-Luc, 1999, "Heidegger's 'Originary Ethics,'" trans. Duncan Large, *Studies in Practical Philosophy* 1(1):12–35.

Safranski, Rüdiger, 1998, *Martin Heidegger: Between Good and Evil*, trans. Ewald Osers. Cambridge, MA: Harvard University Press.

Sale, Stephen and Salisbury, Laura (eds), 2015, *Kittler Now: Current Perspectives in Kittler Studies*. Cambridge: Polity Press.

Sommer, Christian, 2013, *Heidegger 1933: Le programme platonicien du Discours de rectorat*. Paris: Hermann.

Thomä, Dieter, 1990, *Die Zeit des Selbst und die Zeit danach: Zur Kritik der Textgeschichte Martin Heideggers 1910–1976*. Frankfurt am Main: Suhrkamp Verlag.

Trawny, Peter, 2011, *Adyton: Heideggers esoterische Philosophie*. Berlin: Matthes & Seitz.

Trawny, Peter, 2015, *Heidegger and the Myth of a Jewish World Conspiracy*, trans. Andrew Mitchell. Chicago, IL: University of Chicago Press.

Trawny, Peter and Mitchell, Andrew J. (eds) 2015, *Heidegger, die Juden, noch einmal*, Frankfurt am Main: Vittorio Klostermann Verlag.

Vetter, Helmuth, 2014, *Grundriss Heidegger: Ein Handbuch zu Leben und Werk*. Hamburg: Felix Meiner Verlag.

von Herrmann, Friedrich-Wilhelm, 1994, *Wege ins Ereignis: Zu Heideggers 'Beiträgen zur Philosophie'*. Frankfurt am Main: Vittorio Klostermann Verlag.

Zaborowski, Holgar, 2010, *'Eine Frage von Irre und Schuld?': Martin Heidegger und der Nationalsozialismus*. Frankfurt am Main: S. Fischer Verlag.

Zarader, Marlène, 2006, *The Unthought Debt: Heidegger and the Hebraic Heritage*, trans. Bettina Bergo. Stanford, CA: Stanford University Press.

Index